Byways
of
Blessedness

JAMES ALLEN TITLES

Byways
of
Blessedness

James Allen

Published 2019 by Gildan Media LLC
aka G&D Media
www.GandDmedia.com

Design by Meghan Day Healey of Story Horse, LLC

Library of Congress Cataloging-in-Publication Data is available upon request

ISBN: 978-1-7225-0250-8

10   9   8   7   6   5   4   3   2   1

Contents

Foreword

A long the highways of Burma there are placed, at regular distances away from the dust of the road and under the cool shade of groups of trees, small wooden buildings called "rest-houses," where the weary traveller may rest a while, and allay his thirst and assuage his hunger and fatigue by partaking of the food and the water that the kindly inhabitants place there as a religious duty. Along the great highways of life there are such resting-places; away from the heat of passion and the dust of disappointment, under the cool and refreshing shade of lowly Wisdom, are the humble, unimposing "rest-houses" of peace, and the little, almost unnoticed, byways of blessedness, where alone the weary and footsore can find strength and healing. Nor can these byways be ignored without suffering. Along the great road of life, hurrying, and eager to reach some illusive goal, presses the multitude, despising the apparently insignificant "rest-houses" of true thought, not heeding the narrow little byways of blessed action, regarded by them as unimportant; and hour by hour men are fainting and falling, and numbers that cannot be counted perish of heart-hunger, heart-thirst, and heart-fatigue. But he who will step aside from the passionate press, and deign to enter the byways here presented, his happy feet shall press the incomparable flowers of blessedness, his eyes be gladdened with their beauty, and his mind refreshed with their sweet perfume. Rested and sustained, he shall escape the fever and delirium of life, and, strong and happy, he will not fall fainting in the dust nor perish by the way, but will successfully accomplish his journey.

—James Allen

Right Beginnings

All common things, each day's events,
That with the hour begin and end;
Our pleasures and our discontents
Are rounds by which we may ascend.
We have not wings, we cannot soar;
But we have feet to scale and climb.

–Longfellow

For common life its wants
And ways, would I set forth in beauteous hues.

–Browning

Life is full of beginnings. They are presented every day and every hour to every person. Most beginnings are small and appear trivial and insignificant, but in reality they are the most important things in life.

See how in the material world everything proceeds from small beginnings. The mightiest river is at first a rivulet over which the grasshopper could leap; the great flood commences with a few drops of rain; the sturdy oak, that has endured the storms of a thousand winters, was once an acorn.

Consider how in the spiritual world the greatest things proceed from smallest beginnings. A light fancy may be the inception of a wonderful invention or an immortal work of art; a spoken sentence may turn the tide of history; a pure thought entertained may lead to the exercise of a world-wide regenerative power.

Have you yet discovered the vast importance of beginnings? Do you really know what is involved in a beginning? Do you know the number of beginnings you are continuously making, and do you realize their full import? If not, come with me for a short time, thoughtfully to explore this much ignored byway of blessedness; for blessed it is when wisely resorted to, and much strength and comfort it holds for the understanding mind.

A beginning is a cause, and as such it must be followed by an effect or a train of effects, and the effect will be of the same nature as the cause. The nature of an initial impulse determines the body of its results. A beginning also presupposes an ending, a consummation, achievement, or goal. A gate leads to a path, and the path to some particular destination; so a beginning leads to results, and results lead to a completion.

There are right beginnings and wrong beginnings, followed by effects of a like nature. You can, by careful thought, avoid wrong beginnings and make right beginnings, and so escape evil results and enjoy good results.

There are beginnings over which you have no control and authority—these are without, in the universe, in the world of nature around you, and in other people possessing the same liberty as yourself.

Do not concern yourself with these beginnings, but direct your energies and attention to those beginnings over which you have complete control and authority, which bring about the complicated web of results which compose your life. These beginnings are to be found in the realm of your own thoughts and actions; in your mental attitude toward the variety of circumstances through which you pass; in your conduct day by day—in short, in your life as you make it, which is your world of good or ill.

In aiming at the life of Blessedness one of the simplest beginnings to be considered and rightly made is that which we all make every day—the beginning of each day's life.

How do you begin each day? At what hour do you rise? How do you begin your work? In what frame of mind do you enter upon the sacred life of a new day? What answer can you give your heart to these important questions? You will find that much happiness or unhappiness follows upon the right or wrong beginning of the day, and that, when every day is wisely begun, happy and harmonious sequences will mark its course, and life in its totality will not fall far short of the ideal blessedness.

It is a right and strong beginning of the day to rise at an early hour. Even if your worldly work does not demand it, it is wise to make of it a habit, and begin the day strongly by shaking off indolence and by putting on vigor and energy. How are you to develop strength of will and mind and body if you begin every day by yielding to weakness? Self-indulgence is followed by unhappiness.

Those who lie a-bed till late are not necessarily bright and cheerful and fresh, but often the prey of irritabilities, depressions, debilities, nervous disorders, abnormal fancies, and all unhappy moods.

This is the heavy price they have to pay for their daily indulgence. Yet, so blinding is the pandering to self that, like the man taking his daily dram in the belief that it is bracing the nerves which it is all the time shattering, so the lie-a-bed is convinced that long hours of ease are necessary for him as a possible remedy for those very moods and weaknesses and disorders of which his indulgence is the cause. Men and women are unaware of the losses that they entail upon themselves by this common indulgence: loss of strength both of mind and body, loss of prosperity, loss of knowledge, and loss of happiness.

Begin the day by rising early. If you have no object in doing so, never mind; arise, go for a gentle walk among the beauties of nature, and you will experience a buoyancy, a freshness, and a delight, not to say a peace of mind, that will reward you for your effort. One good effort is followed by another; and when a man begins the day by rising early, even though with no other purpose in view, he will find the silent early hour so conducive to clearness of mind and calmness of thought, his early morning walk so profitable in enabling him to become a consecutive thinker and so to see life and its problems, as well as himself and his affairs, in a clearer light; that in time he will rise early for the express purpose of preparing and harmonizing his mind to meet any and every difficulty with wisdom and calm strength.

There is, indeed, so spiritual an influence in the early morning hour, so divine a silence and inexpressible repose, that he who, purposeful and strong, throws off the mantle of ease and climbs the hills to greet the morning sun will thereby climb no inconsiderable distance up the hills of blessedness and truth.

The right beginning of the day will be followed by cheerfulness at the first meal, permeating the household with a sunny influence; and the work of the day will be undertaken in a strong and confident spirit, and the whole day will be well lived.

There is also a sense in which every day is to be regarded as the beginning of a new life, in which one can think, act, and live newly, and in a wiser and better spirit.

Every day is a fresh beginning;
Every morn is the world made new.
Ye who are weary of sorrow and sinning,
Here is a beautiful hope for you,
A hope for me and a hope for you.

Do not dwell upon the sins and mistakes of yesterday so exclusively as to have no energy and mind left for living rightly today, and do not think that the sins of yesterday can prevent you from living aright today. Begin today right with the world, and aided by the accumulated experiences of all your past days, live it better than any of your previous days; but you cannot possibly live it better unless you begin it better. The character of the whole day depends upon the way it is begun.

Another beginning of great importance is the beginning of any particular and responsible undertaking. How does a man begin the building of a house? He secures a plan of the proposed edifice, and proceeds to build according to the plan, scrupulously following it in every detail, from the foundation up. Should he neglect the beginning—the obtaining of an architectural plan—his labor would be wasted, and his building, should it reach completion without tumbling to pieces, would be insecure and worthless. The same law holds good in any important work: the right beginning and first essential is a definite mental plan on which to build. Nature will have no slip-shod work, no slovenliness, and she annihilates confusion, or rather, confusion is in itself annihilation. Order, definiteness, purpose, eternally and universally prevail; and he who in his operations ignores these elements of precision at once deprives himself of substantiality, completeness, success.

> *Life without a plan,*
> *As useless as the moment it began,*
> *Serves merely as a soil for discontent*
> *To thrive in, an encumbrance ere half spent.*

Let a man start in business without having in his mind a well formed plan to pursue systematically, and he will be incoherent in his efforts and must fail in his business operations. The laws to be observed in the building of a house also operate in the building up of a business. A definite plan is followed by coherent effort; and coherent effort is followed by well-knit and orderly results—completeness, perfection, success, happiness.

But not only mechanical and commercial enterprise—all undertakings, of whatsoever nature, come under this law. The author's book, the artist's picture, the orator's speech, the reformer's work, the inventor's machine, the general's campaign, are all carefully organized and planned in the mind before the attempt to actualize them is commenced; and in accordance with the unity, solidarity, and perfection of the original mental plan will be the actual and ultimate success of the undertaking.

Successful men, influential men, good men are those who, among other things, have learned the value and utilized the power hidden in the obscure beginnings that the foolish man passes by as insignificant.

But the most important beginning of all—that upon which affliction or blessedness inevitably depends, yet the one most neglected and least understood—is the inception of thought in the hidden, but causal, region of the mind. Your whole life is a series of effects, having their cause in thought—in your own thought. All conduct is made and moulded by thought; all deeds, good or bad, are thoughts made visible. A seed put into the ground is the beginning of a plant or tree; the seed germinates, the plant or tree comes forth into the light and evolves. A thought put into the mind is the beginning of a line of conduct: the thought first sends down its roots into the mind, thence to push forth into the light in the form of actions or conduct, which evolve into character and destiny.

Loving, gentle, kind, unselfish, and pure thoughts are right beginnings, leading to blissful results.

This is so simple, so plain, so absolutely true; and yet how neglected, how evaded, and how little understood!

The gardener who most carefully studies how, when, and where to put in his seeds gains the greater horticultural knowledge and obtains the best results. The best crops gladden the soul of him who makes the best beginning. The man who most patiently studies how to put into his mind the seeds of strong, wholesome, and charitable thoughts, will obtain the best results in life, and gain the greater knowledge of truth. The greatest blessedness comes to him who infuses into his mind the purest and noblest thoughts.

None but right acts can follow right thoughts; none but a right life can follow right acts—and by living a right life all blessedness is achieved.

He who considers the nature and import of his thoughts, who strives daily to eliminate bad thoughts and supplant them with good, comes at last to see that thoughts are the beginnings of results which affect every fibre of his being, which potently influence every event and circumstance of his life. And when he thus sees, he thinks only right thoughts, chooses to make only those mental beginnings which lead to peace and blessedness.

Wrong thoughts are painful in their inception, painful in their growth, and painful in their fruitage. Right thoughts are blissful in their inception, blissful in their growth, and blissful in their fruitage.

Many are the right beginnings which a man must discover and adopt on his way to wisdom; but that which is first and last, most important and all-embracing, which is the source and fountain of all abiding happiness, is the right beginning of the mental operations—this implies the steady development of self-control, willpower, steadfastness, strength, purity, gentleness, insight, and comprehension. It leads to the perfecting of life, for he who thinks perfectly has abolished all unhappiness, his every moment is peaceful, his years are rounded with bliss—he has attained to the complete and perfect blessedness.

Small Tasks and Duties

Wrapped in our nearest duty is the key
  Which shall unlock for us the Heavenly Gate:
Unveiled, the Heavenly Vision he shall see.
  Who cometh not too early or too late.

Like the star
That shines afar,
Without haste
And without rest,
Let each man wheel with steady sway
Round the task that rules the day,
And do his best.

—Goethe

As pain and bliss inevitably follow on wrong and right beginnings, so unhappiness and blessedness are inseparably bound up with small tasks and duties. Not that a duty has any power of itself to bestow happiness or the reverse—this is contained in the attitude of mind which is assumed toward the duty—and everything depends upon the way in which it is approached and done.

Not only great happiness but great power arises from doing little things unselfishly, wisely, and perfectly, for life in its totality is made up of little things. Wisdom inheres in the common details of everyday existence, and when the parts are made perfect the Whole will be without blemish.

Everything in the universe is made up of little things, and the perfection of the great is based upon the perfection of the small. If any detail of the universe were imperfect the Whole would be imperfect. If any particle were omitted the aggregate would cease to be. Without a grain of dust there could be no world, and the world is perfect because the grain of dust is perfect. Neglect of the small is confusion of the great. The snowflake is as perfect as the star; the dewdrop is as symmetrical as the planet; the microbe is not less mathematically proportioned than the man. By laying stone upon stone, plumbing and fitting each with perfect adjustment, the temple at last stands forth in all its architectural beauty. The small precedes the great. The small is not merely the apologetic attendant of the great, it is its master and informing genius.

Vain men are ambitious to be great, and look about to do some great thing, ignoring and despising the little tasks which call for immediate attention, and in the doing of which there is no vainglory, regarding such "trivialities" as beneath the notice of great men. The fool lacks knowledge because he lacks humility, and, inflated with the thought of self-importance, he aims at impossible things.

The great man has become such by the scrupulous and unselfish attention which he has given to small duties. He has become wise and powerful by sacrificing ambition and pride in the doing of those necessary things which evoke no applause and promise no reward. He never sought greatness; he sought faithfulness, unselfishness, integrity, truth; and in finding these in the common round of small tasks and duties he unconsciously ascended to the level of greatness.

The great man knows the vast value that inheres in moments, words, greetings, meals, apparel, correspondence, rest, work, detached efforts, fleeting obligations, in the thousand-and-one little things which press upon him for attention—briefly, in the common details of life. He sees everything as divinely apportioned, needing only the application of dispassionate thought and action on his part to render life blessed and perfect. He neglects nothing, does not hurry; seeks to escape nothing but error and folly; attends to every duty as it is presented to him, and does not postpone and regret. By giving himself unreservedly to his nearest duty, forgetting alike pleasure and pain, he attains to that combined childlike simplicity and unconscious power which is greatness.

The advice of Confucius to his disciples: "Eat at your own table as you would at the table of a king," emphasises the immeasurable importance of little things, as also does that aphorism of another great teacher, Buddha: "If anything is to be done, let a man do it, let him attack it vigorously."

To neglect small tasks, or to execute them in a perfunctory or slovenly manner, is a mark of weakness and folly.

The giving of one's entire and unselfish attention to every duty in its proper place evolves, by a natural growth, higher and ever higher combinations of duties, because it evolves power and develops talent, genius, goodness, character. A man ascends into greatness as naturally and unconsciously as the plant evolves a flower, and in the same manner, by fitting with unabated energy and diligence, every effort and detail in its proper place, thus harmonising his life and character without friction or waste of power.

Of the almost innumerable recipes for the development of "will-power" and "concentration" which are now scattered abroad, one looks almost in vain for any wholesome hint applicable to vital experience. "Breathings," "postures," "visualisings," "occult methods" are practices as delusive as they are artificial and remote from all that is real and essential in life; while the true path of—path of duty, of earnest and undivided application to one's daily task—along which alone will-power and concentration of thought can be wholesomely and normally developed, remains unknown, untrodden, unexplored even by the elect.

All unnatural forcing and straining in order to gain "power" should be abandoned. There is no way from childhood to manhood but by growth; nor is there any other way from folly to wisdom, from ignorance to knowledge, from weakness to strength. A man must learn how to grow little by little and day after day, by adding thought to thought, effort to effort, deed to deed.

It is true the fakir gains some sort of power by his long persistence in "postures," and "mortifications," but it is a power which is bought at a heavy price, and that price is an equal loss of strength in another direction. He is never a strong, useful character, but a mere fantastic specialist in some psychological trick. He is not a developed man, he is a maimed man.

True will-power consists in overcoming the irritabilities, follies, rash impulses, and moral lapses which accompany the daily life of the individual, and which are apt to manifest themselves on every slight provocation; and in developing calmness, self-possession, and dispassionate action in the press and heat of worldly duties, and in the midst of the passionate and unbalanced throng.

Anything short of this is not true power, and this can only be developed along the normal pathway of steady growth in executing ever more and more masterfully, unselfishly, and perfectly the daily round of legitimate tasks and pressing obligations.

The master is not he whose "psychological accomplishments," rounded by mystery and wonder, leave him in unguarded moments the prey of irritability, of regret, of peevishness, or other petty folly or vice, but he whose "mastery" is manifested in fortitude, non-resentment, steadfastness, calmness, and Infinite patience. The true Master is master of himself; anything other than this is not mastery but delusion.

The man who sets his whole mind on the doing of each task as it is presented, who puts into it energy and intelligence, shutting all else out from his mind, and striving to do that one thing, no matter how small, completely and perfectly, detaching himself from all reward in his task—that man will every day be acquiring greater command over his mind, and will, by ever-ascending degrees, become at last a man of power—a Master.

Put yourself unreservedly into your present task, and so work, so act, so live that you shall leave each task a finished piece of labor—this is the true way to the acquisition of will-power, concentration of thought, and conservation of energy. Look not about for magical formulas, for strained and artificial methods. Every resource is already with you and within you. You have but to learn how wisely to apply yourself in that place which you now occupy. Until this is done those other and higher places which are waiting for you cannot be taken possession of, cannot be reached.

There is no way to strength and wisdom but by acting strongly and wisely in the present moment, and each present moment reveals its own task. The great man, the wise man, does small things greatly, regarding nothing as "trivial" that is necessary. The weak man, the foolish man, does small things carelessly and meanly, hankering the while after some greater work for which, in his neglect and inability in small matters, he is ceaselessly advertising his incapacity. The man who least governs himself is always more ambitious to govern others and assume important responsibilities.

"Whoso neglects a thing which he suspects he ought to do because it seems too small a thing is deceiving himself; it is not too little but too great for him that he doeth it not."

And just as the strong doing of small tasks leads to greater strength, so the doing of those tasks weakly leads to greater weakness. What a man is in his fractional duties that he is in the aggregate of his character. Weakness is as great a source of suffering as sin, and there can be no true blessedness until some measure of strength of character is evolved. The weak man becomes strong by attaching value to little things and doing them accordingly. The strong man becomes weak by falling into looseness and neglect concerning small things, thereby forfeiting his simple wisdom and squandering his energy. Herein we see the beneficent operation of that law of growth which is expressed in the little-understood words: "To him that hath shall be given, and from him that hath not shall be taken away even that which he hath." Man instantly gains or loses by every thought he thinks, every word he says, every act he does, and every work to which he puts hand and heart.

His character from moment to moment is a graduating quantity, to or from which some measure of good is added or subtracted during every moment, and the gain or loss is involved, even to absoluteness, in each thought, word, and deed as these follow each other in rapid sequence.

He who masters the small becomes the rightful possessor of the great. He who is mastered by the small can achieve no superlative victory.

Life is a kind of co-operative trust in which the whole is of the nature of, and dependent upon, the unit.

A successful business, a perfect machine, a glorious temple, or a beautiful character is evolved from the perfect adjustment of a multiplicity of parts.

The foolish man thinks that little faults, little indulgences, little sins, are of no consequence; he persuades himself that so long as he does not commit flagrant immoralities he is virtuous, and even holy; but he is thereby deprived of virtue and holiness, and the world knows him accordingly; it does not reverence, adore, and love him; it passes him by; he is reckoned of no account; his influence is destroyed. The efforts of such a man to make the world virtuous, his exhortations to his fellow-men to abandon great vices, are empty of substance and barren of fruitage. The insignificance which he attaches to his small vices permeates his whole character and is the measure of his manhood: he is regarded as an insignificant man. The levity with which he commits his errors and publishes his weakness comes back to him in the form of neglect and loss of influence and respect: he is not sought after, for who will seek to be taught of folly? His work does not prosper, for who will lean upon a reed? His words fall upon deaf ears, for they are void of practice, wisdom, and experience, and who will go after an echo?

The wise man, or he who is becoming wise, sees the danger which lurks in those common personal faults which men mostly commit thoughtlessly and with impunity; he also sees the salvation which inheres in the abandonment of those faults, as well as in the practice of virtuous thoughts and acts which the majority disregard as unimportant, and in those quiet but momentous daily conquests over self which are hidden from other's eyes.

He who regards his smallest delinquencies as of the gravest nature becomes a saint. He sees the far-reaching influence, good or bad, which extends from his every thought and act, and how he himself is made or unmade by the soundness or unsoundness of those innumerable details of conduct which combine to form his character and life, and so he watches, guards, purifies, and perfects himself little by little and step by step.

As the ocean is composed of drops, the earth of grains, and the stars of points of light, so is life composed of thoughts and acts; without these life would not be. Every man's life, therefore, is what his apparently detached thoughts and acts make it. Their combination is himself. As the year consists of a given number of sequential moments, so a man's character and life consists of a given number of sequential thoughts and deeds, and the finished whole will bear the impress of the parts.

All sorts of things and weather
Must be taken in together,
To make up a year
And a sphere.

Little kindnesses, generosities, and sacrifices make up a kind and generous character. Little renunciations, endurances and victories over self make up a strong and noble character. The truly honest man is honest in the minutest details of his life. The noble man is noble in every little thing he says and does.

It is a fatal delusion with men to think that life is detached from the momentary thought and act, and not to understand that the passing thought and deed is the foundation and substance of life. When this is fully understood all things are seen as sacred, and every act becomes religious. Truth is wrapped up in Infinitesimal details. Thoroughness is genius.

Possessions vanish, and opinions change,
And passions hold a fluctuating seat:
But, by the storms or circumstance unshaken,
And subject neither to eclipse nor wane,
Duty exists.

You do not live your life in the mass; you live it in the fragments, and from these the mass emerges. You can will to live each fragment nobly if you choose, and, this being done, there can be no particle of baseness in the finished whole. The saying "Take care of the pence and the pounds will take care of themselves" is seen to be more than worldly-wise when applied spiritually, for, to take care of the present, passing act, knowing that by so doing the total sum and amount of life and character will be safely preserved, is to be divinely wise. Do not long to do great and laudable things; these will do themselves if you do your present task nobly. Do not chafe at the restrictions and limitations of your present duty, but be nobly unselfish in the doing of it, putting aside discontent, listlessness, and the foolish contemplation of great deeds which lie beyond you—and lo! already the greatness for which you sighed begins to appear. There is no weakness like peevishness. Aspire to the attainment of inward nobility, not outward glory, and begin to attain it where you now are.

The irksomeness and sting which you feel to be in your task are in your mind only. Alter your attitude of mind toward it, and at once the crooked path is made straight, the unhappiness is turned into joy.

See that your every fleeting moment is strong, pure, and purposeful; put earnestness and unselfishness into every passing task and duty; make your every thought, word, and deed sweet and true; thus learning, by practice and experience, the inestimable value of the small things of life, you will gather, little by little, abundant and enduring blessedness.

Transcending Difficulties and Perplexities

Man who would be
Must rule the empire of himself; in it
Must be supreme, establishing his throne
On vanquished will, quelling the anarchy
Of hopes and fears, being himself alone.

–Shelley

Have you missed in your aim? Well, the mark
is still shining.
Did you faint in the race? Well, take breath for
the next.

–Ella Wheeler Wilcox

To suggest that any degree of blessedness may be extracted from difficulties and perplexities will doubtless appear absurd to many; but truth is ever paradoxical, and the curses of the foolish are the blessings of the wise. Difficulties arise in ignorance and weakness, and they call for the attainment of knowledge and the acquisition of strength.

As understanding is acquired by right living, difficulties become fewer, and perplexities gradually fade away, like the perishable mists which they are.

Your difficulty is not contained, primarily, in the situation which gave rise to it, but in the mental state with which you regard that situation and which you bring to bear upon it. That which is difficult to a child presents no difficulty to the matured mind of the man; and that which to the mind of an unintelligent man is surrounded with perplexity would afford no ground for perplexity to an intelligent man.

To the untutored and undeveloped mind of the child how great, and apparently insurmountable, appear the difficulties which are involved in the learning of some simple lesson. How many anxious and laborious hours and days, or even months, its solution costs; and, frequently, how many tears are shed in hopeless contemplation of the unmastered, and apparently insurmountable, wall of difficulty! Yet the difficulty is in the ignorance of the child only, and its conquest and solution is absolutely necessary for the development of intelligence and for the ultimate welfare, happiness, and useful-ness of the child.

Even so is it with the difficulties of life with which older children are confronted, and which it is imperative, for their own growth and develop-ment, that they should solve and surmount; and each difficulty solved means so much more expe-rience gained, so much more insight and wisdom acquired; it means a valuable lesson learned, with the added gladness and freedom of a task success-fully accomplished.

What is the real nature of a difficulty? Is it not a situation which is not fully grasped and understood in all its bearings? As such, it calls for the develop-ment and exercise of a deeper insight and broader intelligence than has hitherto been exercised. It is an urgent necessity calling forth unused energy, and demanding the expression and employment of latent power and hidden resources. It is, therefore, a good angel, albeit disguised; a friend, a teacher; and, when calmly listened to and rightly understood, leads to larger blessedness and higher wisdom.

Without difficulties there could be no progress, no unfoldment, no evolution; universal stagna-tion would prevail, and humanity would perish of ennui.

Let a man rejoice when he is confronted with obstacles, for it means that he has reached the end of some particular line of indifference or folly, and is now called upon to summon up all his energy and intelligence in order to extricate himself, and to find a better way; that the powers within him are crying out for greater freedom, for enlarged exercise and scope.

No situation can be difficult of itself; it is the lack of insight into its intricacies and the want of wisdom in dealing with it, which give rise to the difficulty. Immeasurable, therefore, is the gain of a difficulty transcended.

Difficulties do not spring into existence arbitrarily and accidentally; they have their causes, and are called forth by the law of evolution itself, by the growing necessities of the man's being. Herein resides their blessedness.

There are ways of conduct which end inevitably in complications and perplexities, and there are ways of conduct which lead, just as inevitably, out of troublesome complexities. Howsoever tightly a man may have bound himself round he can always unbind himself. Into whatsoever morasses of trouble and trackless wastes of perplexity he may have ignorantly wandered he can always find his way out of them, can always recover the lost highway of uninvolved simplicity which leads, straight and clear, to the sunny city of wise and blessed action. But he will never do this by sitting down and weeping in despair, nor by complaining and worrying and aimlessly wishing he were differently situated. His dilemma calls for alertness, logical thought, and calm calculation. His position requires that he shall strongly command himself; that he shall think and search, and rouse himself to strenuous and unremitting exertion in order to regain himself. Worry and anxiety only serve to heighten the gloom and exaggerate the magnitude of the difficulty. If he will but quietly take himself to task, and retrace, in thought, the more or less intricate way by which he has come to his present position, he will soon perceive where he made mistakes; will discover those places where hc took a false turn, and where a little more thoughtfulness, judgment, economy, or self-denial would have saved him. He will see how, step by step, he has involved himself, and how a riper judgment and clearer wisdom would have enabled him to take an altogether different and truer course. Having proceeded thus far, and extracted from his past conduct this priceless grain of golden wisdom, his difficulty will already have assumed less impregnable proportions, and he will then be able to bring to bear upon it the searchlight of dispassionate thought, thoroughly to anatomize it, to comprehend it in all its details, and to perceive the relation which those details bear to the motive source of action and conduct within himself. This being done, the difficulty will have ceased, for the straight way out of it will plainly appear, and the man will thus have learned, for all time, his lesson; will have gained an item of wisdom and a measure of blessedness of which he can never again be deprived.

Just as there are ways of ignorance, selfishness, folly, and blindness which end in confusion and perplexity, so there are ways of knowledge, self-denial, wisdom, and insight which lead to pleasant and peaceful consummations. He who knows this will meet difficulties in a courageous spirit, and, in overcoming them, will evolve truth out of error, bliss out of pain, and peace out of perturbation.

No man can be confronted with a difficulty which he has not the strength to meet and subdue. Worry is not merely useless, it is folly, for it defeats that power and intelligence which is otherwise equal to the task. Every difficulty can be overcome if rightly dealt with; anxiety is, therefore, unnecessary. The task which cannot be overcome ceases to be a difficulty, and becomes an impossibility; and anxiety is still unnecessary, for there is only one way of dealing with an impossibility—namely, to submit to it. The inevitable is the best.

Heartily know,
When half-gods go,
The gods arrive.

And just as domestic, social, and economic difficulties are born of ignorance and lead to riper knowledge, so every religious doubt, every mental perplexity, every heart-beclouding shadow, presages greater spiritual gain, is prophetic of a brighter dawn of intelligence for him on whom it falls.

It is a great day in the life of a man (though at the time he knows it not) when bewildering perplexities concerning the mystery of life take possession of his mind, for it signifies that his era of dead indifference, of animal sloth, of mere vegetative happiness, has come to an end, and that henceforth he is to live as an aspiring, self-evolving being. No longer a mere human animal, he will now begin to live as a man, exerting all his mental energies to the solution of life's problems, to the answering of those haunting perplexities which are the sentinels of truth, and which stand at the gate and threshold of the Temple of Wisdom.

He it is who, when great trials come,
Nor seeks nor shuns them, but doth calmly stay.

Nor will he ever rest again in selfish ease and listless ignorance; nor sleekly sate himself upon the swine's husks of fleshly pleasures; nor find a hiding-place from the ceaseless whisperings of his heart's dark and indefinable interrogatories. The divine within him has awakened; a sleeping god is shaking off the incoherent visions of the night, never again to slumber, never again to rest until his eyes rest upon the full, broad day of Truth.

It is impossible for such a man to hush, for any length of time, the call to higher purposes and achievements which is aroused within him, for the awakened faculties of his being will ceaselessly urge him on to the unravelling of his perplexities; for him there is no more peace in sin, no more rest in error, no final refuge but in Wisdom.

Great will be the blessedness of such a man when, conscious of the ignorance of which his doubts and perplexities are born, and acknowledging and understanding that ignorance, not striving to hide himself from it, he earnestly applies himself to its removal, seeks unremittingly, day after day, for that pathway of light which shall enable him to dispel all the dark shadows, dissolve his doubts, and find the solution to all his pressing problems. And as a child is glad when it has mastered a lesson long toiled over, just so a man's heart becomes light and free when he has satisfactorily met some worldly difficulty; even so, but to a far greater degree, is the heart of a man rendered joyous and peaceful when some vital and eternal question which has been long brooded over and grappled with is at last completely answered, and its darkness is forever dispelled.

Do not regard your difficulties and perplexities as portentous of ill; by so doing you will make them ill; but regard them as prophetic of good, which, indeed, they are. Do not persuade yourself that you can evade them; you cannot. Do not try to run away from them; this is impossible, for wherever you go they will still be there with you—but meet them calmly and bravely; confront them with all the dispassion and dignity which you can command; weigh up their proportions; analyse them; grasp their details; measure their strength; understand them; attack them, and finally vanquish them. Thus will you develop strength and intelligence; thus will you enter one of those byways of blessedness which are hidden from the superficial gaze.

Burden-Dropping

This to me is life;
That it life be a burden, I will join
To make it but the burden of a song.
                                        –Bailey

Have you heard that it was good to gain
    the day?
I also say it is good to fall, battles are lost
    in the same spirit in which they are won.
                                        –Walt Whitman

We hear and read much about burden-bearing, but of the better way of burden-dropping very little is heard or known. Yet why should you go about with an oppressive weight at your heart when you might relieve yourself of it and move amongst your fellows heart-free and cheerful? No man carries a load upon his back except necessarily to transfer something from one place to another; he does not saddle his shoulders with a perpetual burden, and then regard himself as a martyr for his pains; and why should you impose upon your mind a useless burden, and then add to its weight the miseries of self-condolence and self-pity? Why not abandon both your load and your misery, and thus add to the gladness of the world by first making yourself glad? No reason can justify, and no logic support, the ceaseless carrying of a grievous load. As in things material a load is only undertaken as a necessary means of transference, and is never a source of sorrow; so in things spiritual a burden should only be taken up as a means toward some good and necessary end, which, when attained, the burden is put aside; and the carrying of such a burden, far from being a source of grief, would be a cause for rejoicing.

We say that bodily mortifications which some religious ascetics inflict upon themselves are unnecessary and vain; and are the mental mortifications which so many people inflict upon themselves less unnecessary and vain?

Where is the burden which should cause unhappiness or sorrow? It does not exist. If a thing is to be done let it be done cheerfully, and not with inward groanings and lamentations. It is of the highest wisdom to embrace necessity as a friend and guide. It is of the greatest folly to scowl upon necessity as an enemy, and to wish or try to overcome or avoid her. We meet our own at every turn, and duties only become oppressive loads when we refuse to recognise and embrace them. He who does any necessary thing in a niggardly and complaining spirit, hunting the while after unnecessary pleasures, lashes himself with the scorpions of misery and disappointment, and imposes upon himself a doubly-weighted burden of weariness and unrest under which he incessantly groans.

> *Wake thou, O self, to better things;*
> *To yonder heights uplift thy wings;*
> *Take up the psalm of life anew;*
> *Sing of the good, sing of the true;*
> *Sing of full victory o'er wrong;*
> *Make thou a richer, sweeter song;*
> *Out of thy doubting, care, and pain*
> *Weave thou a joyous, glad refrain;*
> *Out of thy thorns a crown weave thou*
> *Of rare rejoicing. Sing thou, now.*

I will give my cheerful, unselfish and undivided attention to the doing of all those things which enter into my compact with life, and, though I walk under colossal responsibilities, I shall be unconscious of any troublesome weight or grievous burden.

You say a certain thing (a duty, a companion-ship, or a social obligation) troubles you, is bur-densome, and you resign yourself to oppression with the thought: "I have entered into this, and will go through with it, but it is a heavy and griev-ous work." But is the thing really burdensome, or is it your selfishness that is oppressing you? I tell you that that very thing which you regard as so imprisoning a restriction is the first gateway to your emancipation; that work which you regard as a perpetual curse contains for you the actual bless-edness which you vainly persuade yourself lies in another and unapproachable direction. All things are mirrors in which you see yourself reflected, and the gloom which you perceive in your work is but a reflection of that mental state which you bring to it. Bring a right, unselfish, state of heart to the thing, and lo! it is at once transformed, and becomes a means of strength and blessedness, reflecting back that which you have brought to it. If you bring a scowling face to your looking-glass will you complain of the glass that it glowers upon you with a deformed visage, or will you put your face right, and so get back from the reflector a more pleasing countenance?

If it is right and necessary that a thing should be done then the doing of it is good, and it can only become burdensome in wishing not to do it.

The selfish wish makes the thing appear evil. If it is neither right nor necessary that a thing should be done then the doing of it in order to gain some coveted pleasure is folly, which can only lead to burdensome issues.

The duty which you shirk is your reproving angel; the pleasure which you race after is your flattering enemy. Foolish man! when will you turn round and be wise?

It is the beneficence of the universe that it is everywhere, and at all times, urging its creatures to wisdom as it demands coherence of its atoms. That folly and selfishness entail suffering in ever-increasing degrees of intensity is preservative and good, for agony is the enemy of apathy and the herald of wisdom.

What is painful? What is grievous? What is burdensome? Passion is painful; folly is grievous; selfishness is burdensome.

It is the dark idolatry of self
Which, when our thoughts and actions once
*   are done,*
Demands that man should weep, and bleed,
*   and groan.*

Eliminate passion, folly, and selfishness from your mind and conduct and you will eliminate suffering from your life. Burden-dropping consists in abandoning the inward selfishness and putting pure love in its place. Go to your task with love in your heart and you will go to it light-hearted and cheerful.

The mind, through ignorance, creates its own burdens and inflicts its own punishments. No one is doomed to carry any load. Sorrow is not arbitrarily imposed. These things are self-made.

Reason is the rightful monarch of the mind, and anarchy reigns in his spiritual kingdom when his throne is usurped by passion. When love of pleasure is to the fore heaviness and anguish compose the rear. You are free to choose. Even if you are bound by passion, and feel helpless, you have bound yourself, and are not helpless. Where you have bound you can unbind. You have come to your present state by degrees, and you can recover yourself by degrees, can reinstate reason and dethrone passion. The time to avoid evil is before pleasure is embraced, but, once embraced, its train of consequences should teach you wisdom. The time to decide is before responsibilities are adopted, but, once adopted, all selfish considerations, with their attendant grumblings, whinings, and complainings, should be religiously excluded from the heart. Responsibilities lose their weight when carried lovingly and wisely.

What heavy burden is a man weighted with which is not made heavier and more unendurable by weak thoughts or selfish desires? If your circumstances are "trying" it is because you need them, and can evolve the strength to meet them. They are trying because there is some weak spot within you, and they will continue to be trying until that spot is eradicated. Be glad that you have the opportunity of becoming stronger and wiser. No circumstances can be trying to wisdom; nothing can weary love. Stop brooding over your own trying circumstances and contemplate the lives of some of those about you.

Here is a woman with a large family who has to make ends meet on a pound a week. She performs all her domestic duties, down to the washing, finds time to attend on sick neighbors, and manages to keep entirely out of the two common quagmires—debt and despondency. She is cheerful from morning to night, and never complains of her "trying circumstances." She is perennially cheerful because she is unselfish. She is happy in the thought that she is the means of happiness to others. Were she to brood upon the holidays, the pretty baubles, the lazy hours of which she is deprived; of the plays she cannot see, the music she cannot hear, the books she cannot read, the parties she cannot attend, the good she might do, the friendships she is debarred from forming; of the many pleasures which might only be hers if her circumstances were more favorable—if she brooded thus what a miserable creature she would be! How unbearably laborious her work would become! How every little domestic duty would hang like a millstone about her neck, dragging her down to the grave which, unless she altered her state of mind, she would quickly reach, killed by—selfishness! But, not living in vain desires for herself, she is relieved of all burdens, and is happy. Cheerfulness and unselfishness are sworn friends. Love knows no heavy toil.

Here is another woman, with a private income which is more than sufficient, combined with leisure and luxury, yet, because she is called upon to forfeit a portion of her time, pleasure, and money to discharge some obligation which she wishes to be rid of, and which should be to her a work of loving service, or fostering in her heart some ungratified desire, she is perpetually discontented and unhappy, and complains of "trying circumstances." Discontent and selfishness are inseparable companions. Self-love knows no joyful labor.

Of the two sets of circumstances above depicted (and life is crowded with such contrasted instances) which are the "trying" conditions? Is it not true that neither of them are trying, and that both are blest or unblest in accordance with the measure of love or selfishness which is infused into them? Is not the root of the whole matter in the mind of the individual and not in the circumstance?

When a man, who has recently taken up the study of some branch of theology, religion, or "occultism," says; "If I had not burdened myself with a wife and family I could have done a great work; and had I known years ago what I know now I would never have married," I know that that man has not yet found the commonest and broadest way of wisdom (for there is no greater folly than regret,) and that he is incapable of the great work which he is so ambitious to perform. If a man has such deep love for his fellow-men that he is anxious to do a great work for humanity he will manifest that surpassing love always and in the place where he now is. His home will be filled with it, and the beauty and sweetness and peace of his unselfish love will follow wherever he goes, making happy those about him and transmuting all things into good. The love that goes abroad to air itself, and is undiscoverable at home, is not love—it is vanity.

Have I not seen (Oh, pitiful sight!) the cheerless home and neglected children of the misguided missioner and religionist? It is on such self-delusion as this that self-pity and self-martyrdom ever wait, and its self-inflicted misery is regarded by the deluded one as a holy and religious burden which he or she is called upon to bear.

Only a great man can do a great work; and he will be great wherever he is, and will do his noble work under whatsoever conditions he may find himself when he has unfolded and revealed that work.

Thou who art so anxious to work for humanity, to help thy fellow-men, begin that work at home; help thyself, thy neighbor, thy wife, thy child. Do not be deluded; until thou doest, with utmost faithfulness, the nearer and the lesser thou canst not do the farther and greater.

If a man has lived many years of his life in lust and selfish pleasure it is in the order of things that his accumulated errors should at last weigh heavily upon him, as, until they are thus brought home to him, he will not abandon them, will not exert himself to find a better life; but whilst he regards his self-made, self-imposed burdens as "holy crosses" imposed upon him by the Supreme, or as marks of superior virtue, or as loads which Fate, circumstances, or other people have heaped undeservedly and unjustly upon him, he is but lengthening out his folly, increasing the weight of his burdens, and multiplying his pains and sorrows. Only when such a man wakes up to the truth that his burdens are of his own making, that they are the accumulated effects of his own acts, will he cease from unmanly self-pity and find the better way of burden-dropping; only when he opens his eyes to see that his every thought and act is another brick, another stone, built into the temple of his life will he develop the insight which will enable him to recognise his own unstable handiwork, the unflinching manliness to acknowledge it, and the courage to build more nobly and enduringly.

Painful burdens are necessary, but only so long as we lack love and wisdom.

The Temple of Blessedness lies beyond the outer courts of suffering and humiliation and to reach it the pilgrim must pass through the outer courts. For a time he will linger in the outer, but only so long as, through his own imperfect understanding, he mistakes it for the inner. While he pities himself and confounds suffering with holiness he will remain in suffering; but when, casting off the last unholy rag of self-pity, he perceives that suffering is a means and not an end, that it is a state self-originated and self-propagated, then converted and right-minded, he will rapidly pass through the outer courts, and reach the inner abode of peace.

Suffering does not originate in the perfect but in the imperfect; it does not mark the complete but the incomplete; it can, therefore, be transcended.

Its self-born cause can be found, investigated, comprehended, and for ever removed.

It is true, therefore, that we must pass through agony to rest, through loneliness to peace; but let the sufferer not forget that it *is* a "passing through;" that the agony is a gateway and not a habitation; that the loneliness is a pathway and not a destination; and that a little farther on he will come to the painless and blissful repose.

Little by little is a burden accumulated; imperceptibly and by degrees is its weight increased. A thoughtless impulse, a gross self-indulgence, a blind passion yielded to and gratified again and again; an impure thought fostered, a cruel word uttered, a foolish thing done time after time, and at last the gathered weight of many follies becomes oppressive. At first, and for a time, the weight is not felt; but it is being added to day after day, and the time comes when the accumulated burden is felt in all its galling weight, when the bitter fruits of selfishness are gathered, and the heart is troubled with the weariness of life. When this period arrives let the sufferer look to himself; let him search for the blessed way of burden-dropping, finding which he will find wisdom to live better, purity to live sweeter, love to live nobler: will find, in the reversal of that conduct by which his burdens were accumulated, light-hearted nights and days, cheerful action, and unclouded joy.

Come out of the world—come above it—
    Up over its crosses and graves;
Though the green earth is fair and I love it,
    We must love it as masters, not slaves.
Come up where the dust never rises—
    But only the perfume of flowers—
And your life shall be glad with surprises
    Of beautiful hours.

Hidden Sacrifices

What need hath man
Of Eden passed, or Paradise to come,
When heaven is round us and within ourselves?

Lowliness is the base of every virtue:
Who goes the lowest, builds, doubt not, the
   safest.

   –Bailey

Truth is within ourselves; it takes no rise
From outward things, whate'er you may
   believe.

   –Browning

It is one of the paradoxes of Truth that we gain by giving up; we lose by greedily grasping. Every gain in virtue necessitates some loss in vice; every accession of holiness means some selfish pleasure yielded up; and every forward step on the path of

Truth demands the forfeit of some self-assertive error.

He who would be clothed in new garments must first cast away the old, and he who would find the True must sacrifice the false. The gardener digs in the weeds in order that they may feed, with their decay, the plants which are good for food; and the Tree of Wisdom can only flourish on the compost of uprooted follies. Growth—gain—necessitates sacrifice—loss.

The true life, the blessed life, the life that is not tormented with passions and pains, is reached only through sacrifice, not necessarily the sacrifice of outward things, but the sacrifice of the inward errors and defilements, for it is these, and these only, which bring misery into life. It is not the good and true that needs to be sacrificed but the evil and false; therefore all sacrifice is ultimately gain, and there is no essential loss. Yet at first the loss seems great, and the sacrifice is painful, but this is because of the self delusion and spiritual blindness which always accompany selfishness, and pain must always accompany the cutting away of some selfish portion of one's nature. When the drunkard resolves to sacrifice his lust for strong drink he passes through a period of great suffering, and he feels that he is forfeiting a great pleasure; but when his victory is complete, when the lust is dead, and his mind is calm and sober, then he knows that he has gained incalculably by the giving up of his selfish animal pleasure. What he has lost was evil and false, and not worth keeping—nay, its keeping entailed continual misery—but what he has gained, in character, in self-control, in soberness and greater peace of mind, is good and true, and it was necessary that he should acquire it.

So it is with all true sacrifice; it is at first, and until it is completed, painful, and this is why men shrink from it. They cannot see any purpose in abstaining from and overcoming selfish gratification; it seems to them like losing so much that is sweet, seems to them like courting misery, and giving up all happiness and pleasure. And this must be so; for if a man could know that by giving up his particular forms of selfishness his gain in happiness would be immeasurably greater, unselfishness (which is now so difficult of attainment) would then be rendered Infinitely more difficult of achievement, for his desire for the greater gain his selfishness—would thereby be greatly intensified.

No man can become unselfish, and thereby arrive at the highest bliss, until he is willing to lose, looking for neither gain nor reward: it is this state of mind which constitutes unselfishness. A man must be willing humbly to sacrifice his selfish habits and practices because they are untrue and unworthy, and for the happiness of those about him, without expecting any reward or looking for any good to accrue to himself; nay, he must be prepared to lose for himself, to forfeit pleasure and happiness, even life itself, if by so doing he can make the world more beautiful and happy. But does he lose? Does the miser lose when he gives up his lust for gold? Does the thief lose when he abandons stealing? Does the libertine lose when he sacrifices his unworthy pleasures? No man loses by the sacrifice of self, or some portion of self; nevertheless he thinks he will lose by so doing, and because he so thinks he suffers, and this is where the sacrifice comes in—this is where he gains by losing.

All true sacrifice is within; it is spiritual and hidden, and is prompted by deep humility of heart. Nothing but the sacrifice of self can avail, and to this must all men come sooner or later during their spiritual evolution. But in what does this self-abnegation consist? How is it practised? Where is it sought and found? It consists in overcoming the daily proneness to selfish thoughts and acts; it is practised in our common intercourse with others; and it is found in the hour of tumult and temptation.

There are hidden sacrifices of the heart which are Infinitely blessed both to him that makes them and those for whom they are made, albeit their making costs much effort and some pain. Men are anxious to do some great thing, to perform some great sacrifice which lies beyond the necessities of their experience, while all the time, perhaps, they are neglecting the one thing needful, are blind to that sacrifice which by its very nearness is rendered imperative. Where lurks your besetting sin? Where lies your weakness? Where does temptation assail you most strongly? There shall you make your first sacrifice, and shall find thereby the way unto your peace. Perhaps it is anger or unkindness. Are you prepared to sacrifice the angry impulse and word, the unkind thought and deed? Are you prepared silently to endure abuse, attack, accusation, and unkindness, refusing to pay back these in their own coin? Nay, more, are you prepared to give in return for these dark follies kindness and loving protection? If so, then you are ready to make those hidden sacrifices which lead to beatific bliss.

If you are given to anger or unkindness offer it up. These hard, cruel, and wrong conditions of mind never brought you any good; they can never bring you anything but unrest, misery, and spiritual blindness. Nor can they ever bring to others anything but unhappiness. Perhaps you will say: "But he was unkind to me first; he treated me unjustly." Perhaps so, but what a poor excuse is this! What an unmanly and ineffectual refuge!

For if his unkindness toward you is so wrong and hurtful yours to him must be equally so. Because another is unkind to you is no justification of your own unkindness, but is rather a call for the exercise of greater kindness on your part. Can the pouring in of more water prevent a flood? Neither can unkindness lessen unkindness. Can fire quench fire? Neither can anger overcome anger.

Offer up all unkindness, all anger. "It takes two to make a quarrel;" don't be the "other one." If one is angry or unkind to you try to find out where you have acted wrongly; and, whether you have acted wrongly or not, do not throw back the angry word or unkind act. Remain silent, self-contained, and kindly disposed; and learn, by continual effort in right-doing, to have compassion upon the wrong-doer.

Perhaps you are habitually impatient and irritable. Know, then, the hidden sacrifice which is needful that you should make. Give up your impatience. Overcome it there where it is wont to assert itself. Resolve that you will yield no longer to its tyrannical sway but will conquer it and cast it out. It is not worth keeping a single hour, nor would it dominate you for another moment if you were not laboring under the delusion that the follies and perversities of others render impatience on your part necessary. Whatever others may do or say, even though they may mock and taunt you, impatience is not only unnecessary, it can never do any other than aggravate the evil which it seeks to remove. Calm, strong, and deliberate action can accomplish much, but impatience and its accompanying irritability are always indications of weakness and inefficiency. And what do they bestow upon you? Do they bestow rest, peace, happiness, or bring these to those about you? Do they not, rather, make you and those about you wretched? But though your impatience may hurt others it certainly hurts and wounds and impoverishes yourself most of all.

Nor can the impatient man know aught of true blessedness, for he is a continual source of trouble and unrest to himself. The calm beauty and perpetual sweetness of patience are unknown to him, and peace cannot draw near to soothe and comfort him.

There is no blessedness anywhere until impatience is sacrificed; and the sacrifice means the development of endurance, the practice of forbearance, and the creation of a new and gentler habit of mind. When impatience and irritability are entirely put away, are finally offered up on the altar of unselfishness, then is realised and enjoyed the blessedness of a strong, quiet, and peaceful mind.

Each hour we think
Of others more than self, that hour we live again,
And every lowly sacrifice we make
For others' good shall make life more than self,
And ope the windows of thy soul to light
From higher spheres. So hail thy lot with joy.

Then there are little selfish indulgences, some of which appear harmless, and are commonly fostered; but no selfish indulgence can be harmless, and men and women do not know what they lose by repeatedly and habitually succumbing to effeminate and selfish gratifications. If the God in man is to rise strong and triumphant, the beast in man must perish. The pandering to the animal nature, even when it appears innocent and seems sweet, leads away from truth and blessedness. Each time you give way to the animal within you, and feed and gratify him, he waxes stronger and more rebellious, and takes firmer possession of your mind, which should be in the keeping of Truth. Not until a man has sacrificed some apparently trivial indulgence does he discover what strength, what joy, what poise of character and holy influence he has all along been losing by that gratification; not until a man sacrifices his hankering for pleasure does he enter into the fulness of abiding joy.

By his personal indulgences a man degrades himself, forfeits self-respect to the extent and frequency of his indulgence, and deprives himself of exemplary influence and the power to accomplish lasting good in his work in the world. He also, by allowing himself to be led by blind desire, increases his mental blindness, and fails of that ultimate clearness of vision, that clarified percipience which pierces to the heart of things and comprehends the real and the true. Animal indulgence is alien to the perception of Truth. By the sacrifice of his indulgences man rises above confusion and doubt, and arrives at the possession of insight and surety.

Sacrifice your cherished and coveted indulgence; fix your mind on something higher, nobler, and more enduring than ephemeral pleasure; live superior to the craving for sense-excitement, and you will live neither vainly nor uncertainly.

Very far-reaching in its effect upon others, and rich with the revelations of Truth for him who makes it, is the sacrifice of self-assertion—the giving up of all interference with the lives, views, or religion of other people, substituting for it an understanding love and sympathy. Self-assertion or opinionativeness is a form of egotism or selfishness most generally found in connection with intellec-

tualism and dialectical skill. It is blindly presump-
tive and uncharitable, and, more often than not, is
regarded as a virtue; but when once the mind has
opened to perceive the way of gentleness and self-
sacrificing love then the ignorance, deformity, and
painful nature of self-assertion become apparent.

The victim of self-assertion, setting up his own
opinions as the standard of right and the measure
of judgment, regards all those as wrong whose
lives and opinions run counter to his own, and,
being eager to put others right, is thereby prevented from putting himself right. His attitude of
mind brings about him opposition and contradic-
tion from people who are anxious to put *him* right,
and this wounds his vanity and makes him miserable, so that he lives in an almost continual fever
of unhappy, resentful, and uncharitable thoughts.
There can be no peace for such a man, no true
knowledge, and no advancement until he sacrifices
his desire to bend others to his own way of thinking and acting. Nor can he understand the hearts
of others, and enter lovingly into their strivings
and aspirations. His mind is cramped and embit-
tered, and he is shut out from all sweet sympathy
and spiritual communion.

He who sacrifices the spirit of self-assertion,
who in his daily contact with others puts aside his
prejudices and opinions, and strives both to learn

from others and to understand them as they are, who allows to others perfect liberty (such as he exercises himself) to choose their own opinions, their own way in life—such a man will acquire a deeper insight, a broader charity, and a richer bliss than he has hitherto experienced, and will strike a byway of blessedness from which he was formerly shut out.

Then there is the sacrifice of greed and all greedy thoughts. The willingness that others should possess rather than we; the not-coveting of things for ourselves but rejoicing that they arc possessed and enjoyed by others, that they bring happiness to others; the ceasing to claim one's "own," and the giving up to others, unselfishly and without malice, that which they exact. This attitude of mind is a source of deep peace and great spiritual strength. It is the sacrifice of *self-interest.*

Material possessions are temporary, and in this sense we cannot truly call them our own—they are merely in our keeping for a short time—but spiritual possessions are eternal and must ever remain with us. Unselfishness is a spiritual possession which is only secured by ceasing to covet material possessions and enjoyments, by ceasing to regard things as for our own special and exclusive pleasure, and by our readiness to yield them up for the good of others.

The unselfish man, even though he finds himself involved in riches, stands aloof, in his mind, from the idea of "exclusive possession," and so escapes the bitterness and fear and anxiety which ever accompany the covetous spirit. He does not regard any of his outward accretions as being too valuable to lose, but he regards the virtue of unselfishness as being too valuable to the world—to suffering humanity—to lose or to cast away.

And who is the blessed man? He who is ever hankering after more possessions, thinking only of the personal pleasure he can get out of them? or he who is ever ready to give up what he has for the good and happiness of others? By greed happiness is destroyed; by not-greed happiness is restored.

Another hidden sacrifice, one of great spiritual beauty and of powerful efficacy in the healing of human sorrows, is the sacrifice of *hatred*—the giving up of all bitter thoughts against others, of all malice, dislike, and resentment. Bitter thoughts and blessedness cannot dwell together. Hatred is a fierce fire that scorches up, in the heart of him who harbors it, all the sweet flowers of peace and happiness, and makes a hell of every place where it comes.

Hatred has many names and many forms but only one essence—namely, burning thoughts of resentment against others. It is sometimes, by its blind votaries, called by the name of religion, causing them to attack, slander, and persecute each other because they will not accept each other's views of life and death, thus filling the earth with miseries and tears.

All resentment, dislike, ill-thinking, and ill-speaking of others is hatred, and where there is hatred there is always unhappiness. No one has conquered hatred while thoughts of resentment toward others spring up in his mind. This sacrifice is not complete until a man can think kindly of those who try to do him wrong. Yet it must be made before true blessedness can be realised and known.

Beyond the hard, cruel, steely gates of hatred waits the divine angel of love, ready to reveal herself to him who will subdue and sacrifice his hateful thoughts, and conduct him to his peace.

Whatever others may say of you, whatever they may do to you, *never take offence*. Do not return hatred with hatred. If another hates you perhaps you have, consciously or unconsciously, failed somewhere in your conduct, or there may be some misunderstanding which the exercise of a little gentleness and reason may remove; but, under all circumstances, "Father, forgive them" is Infinitely better, sweeter, and nobler than "I will have nothing more to do with them." Hatred is so small and poor, so blind and wretched. Love is so great and rich, so far-seeing and blissful.

> *The highest culture is to speak no ill:*
> *The best reformer is the man whose eyes*
> *Are quick to see all beauty and all worth;*
> *And by his own discreet, well-ordered life*
> *Alone reproves the erring.*

Sacrifice all hatred, slay it upon the holy altar of devotion—devotion to others. Think no more of any injury to your own petty self, but see to it that henceforth you injure and wound no other. Open the floodgates of your heart for the inpouring of that sweet, great, beautiful love which embraces all with strong yet tender thoughts of protection and peace, leaving not one, nay, not even he who hates or despises or slanders you, out in the cold.

Then there is the hidden sacrifice of impure desires, of weak self-pity and degrading self-praise, of vanity and pride, for these are unblest attitudes of mind, deformities of heart. He who makes them, one by one, gradually subduing and overcoming them, will, according to the measure of his success, rise above weakness and suffering and sorrow, and will comprehend and enjoy the perfect and imperishable blessedness.

Now, all these hidden sacrifices which are here mentioned are pure, humble heart-offerings. They are made within; are offered up on the sacred, lonely, unseen altar of one's own heart. Not one of them can be made until the fault is first silently acknowledged and confessed. No man can sacrifice an error until he first of all confess (to himself) "I am in error;" when, yielding it up, he will perceive and receive the truth which his error formerly obscured.

"The kingdom of heaven cometh not by observation," and the silent sacrifice of self for the good of others, the daily giving up of one's egotistic tendencies, is not seen and rewarded of men, and brings no loud blazon of popularity and praise. It is hidden away from the eyes of all the world, nay, even from the gaze of those who are nearest to you, for no eyes of flesh can perceive its spiritual beauty. But think not that because it is unperceived it is therefore futile. Its blissful radiance is enjoyed by you, and its power for good over others is great and far-reaching, for though they cannot see it, nor, perhaps, understand it, yet they are unconsciously influenced by it. They will not know what silent battles you are fighting, what eternal victories over self you are achieving, but they will *feel* your altered attitude, your new mind wrought of the fabric of love and loving thoughts, and will share somewhat in its happiness and bliss. They will know nothing of the frequent fierceness of the fight you are waging, of the wounds you receive and the healing balm you apply, of the anguish and the after-peace; but they will know that you have grown sweeter and gentler, stronger and more silently self-reliant, more patient and pure, and that they are rested and helped by your presence. What rewards can compare with this? Beside the fragrant offices of love the praises of men are gross and fulsome, and in the pure flame of a selfless heart the flatteries of the world are turned to ashes. Love is its own reward, its own joy, its own satisfaction; it is the final refuge and resting-place of passion-tortured souls.

The sacrifice of self, and the acquisition of the supreme knowledge and bliss which it confers, is not accomplished by one great and glorious act but by a series of lesser and successive sacrifices in the ordinary life of the world, by a succession of steps in the daily conquest of Truth over selfishness.

He who each day accomplishes some victory over himself, who subdues and puts behind him some unkind thought, some impure desire, some tendency to sin, is every day growing stronger, purer, and wiser, and every dawn finds him nearer to that final glory of Truth which each self-sacrificing act reveals in part.

Look not outside thee nor beyond thee for the light and blessedness of Truth, but look within; thou wilt find it within the narrow sphere of thy duty, even in the humble and hidden sacrifices of thine own heart.

Sympathy

When thy gaze
Turns it on thine own soul, be most severe:
But when it falls upon a fellow-man
Let kindliness control it; and refrain
From that belittling censure that springs forth
From common lips like weeds from marshy soil.
                                   –Ella Wheeler Wilcox

I do ask the wounded person how he feels,
I myself become the wounded person.
                                        –Walt Whitman

We can only sympathise with others in so far as we have conquered ourselves. We cannot think and feel for others while we are engaged in condoling with and pitying ourselves; cannot deal tenderly and lovingly with others while we are anxious for our own pre-eminence or for the exclusive preservation of ourselves, our

opinions, and our own generally. What is sympathy but thoughtfulness for others in the forgetful-
ness of self?

To sympathise with others we must first understand them, and to understand them we must
put away all personal preconceptions concerning
them, and must see them as they are. We must
enter into their inner state and become one with
them, looking through their mental eyes and com-
prehending the range of their experience. You cannot, of course, do this with a being whose wisdom
and experiences are greater than your own; nor
can you do it with any if you regard yourself as
being on a higher plane than others (for egotism
and sympathy cannot dwell together), but you can
practice it with all those who are involved in sins
and sufferings from which you have successfully
extricated yourself, and, though your sympathy
cannot embrace and overshadow the man whose
greatness is beyond you, yet you can place yourself
in such an attitude toward him as to receive the
protection of his larger sympathy, and so make for
yourself an easier way out of the sins and sufferings by which you are still enchained.

Prejudice and ill-will are complete barriers to
the giving of sympathy, while pride and vanity
are total barriers to its reception. You cannot sympathise with a person for whom you have conceived

a hatred; you cannot enjoy the sympathy of one whom you envy. You cannot understand the person whom you dislike, or him for whom, through animal impulse, you have framed an ill-formed affection. You do not, cannot, see him as he is, but see only your own imperfect notions of him; see only a distorted image of him through the exaggerating medium of your ill-grounded opinions.

To see others as they are you must not allow impulsive likes or dislikes, powerful prejudices, or egotistic considerations to come between you and them. You must not resent their actions or condemn their beliefs and opinions. You must leave yourself entirely out, and must, for the time being, assume their position. Only in this way can you become *en rapport* with them, and so fathom their life, their experience, and understand it, and when a man is understood it becomes impossible to condemn him. Men misjudge, condemn, and avoid each other because they do not understand each other, and they do not understand each other because they have not overcome and purified themselves.

Life is growth, development, evolution, and there is no essential distinction between the sinner and the saint—there is only a difference in degree. The saint was once a sinner; the sinner will one day be a saint. The sinner is the child; the saint is the grown man. He who separates himself from sinners, regarding them as wicked men to be avoided, is like a man avoiding contact with little children because they are unwise, disobedient, and play with toys.

All life is one, but it has a variety of manifestations. The grown flower is not something distinct from the tree: it is a part of it; is only another form of leaf. Steam is not something apart from water: it is but another form of water. And in like manner good is transmuted evil: the saint is the sinner developed and transformed.

The sinner is one whose understanding is undeveloped, and he ignorantly chooses wrong modes of action. The saint is one whose understanding is ripened, and he wisely chooses right modes of action. The sinner condemns the sinner, condemnation being a wrong mode of action. The saint never condemns the sinner, remembering that he himself formerly occupied the same place, but thinks of him with deep sympathy, regarding him in the light of a younger brother or a friend, for sympathy is a right and enlightened mode of action.

The perfected saint, who gives sympathy to all, needs it of none, for he has transcended sin and suffering, and lives in the enjoyment of lasting bliss; but all who suffer need sympathy, and all who sin *must* suffer. When a man comes to understand that every sin, whether of thought or deed, receives its just quota of suffering he ceases to condemn and begins to sympathise, seeing the sufferings which sin entails; and he comes to such understanding by purifying himself. As a man purges himself of passions, as he transmutes his selfish desires and puts under foot his egotistic tendencies, he sounds the depths of all human experiences—all sins and sufferings and sorrows, all motives and thoughts and deeds—and comprehends the moral law in its perfection. Complete self-conquest is perfect knowledge, perfect sympathy, and he who views men with the stainless vision of a pure heart views them with a pitying heart, sees them as part of himself, not as something defiled and separate and distinct, but as his very self, sinning as he has sinned, suffering as he has suffered, sorrowing as he has sorrowed, yet, withal, glad in the knowledge that they will come, as he has come, to perfect peace at last.

The truly good and wise man cannot be a passionate partisan, but extends his sympathy to all, seeing no evil in others to be condemned and resisted, but seeing the sin which is pleasant to the sinner, and the after-sorrow and pain which the sinner does not see, and, when it overtakes him, does not understand.

A man's sympathy extends just so far as his wisdom reaches, and no further; and a man only grows wiser as he grows tenderer and more compassionate. To narrow one's sympathy is to narrow one's heart, and so to darken and embitter one's life. To extend and broaden one's sympathy is to enlighten and gladden one's life, and to make plainer to others the way of light and gladness.

To sympathise with another is to receive his being into our own, to become one with him, for unselfish love indissolubly unites, and he whose sympathy reaches out to and embraces all humankind and all living creatures has realised his identity and oneness with all, and comprehends the universal Love and Law and Wisdom.

Man is shut out from Heaven and Peace and Truth only in so far as he shuts out others from his sympathy. Where his sympathy ends his darkness and torment and turmoil begin, for to shut others out from our love is to shut ourselves out from the blessedness of love, and to become cramped in the dark prison of self.

Whoever walks a furlong without sympathy
walks to his own funeral dressed in a shroud.

Only when one's sympathy is unlimited is the Eternal Light of Truth revealed; only in the Love that knows no restrictions is the boundless bliss enjoyed.

Sympathy is bliss; in it is revealed the highest, purest blessedness. It is divine, for in its reciprocal light all thought of self is lost, and there remains only the pure joy of oneness with others, the ineffable communion of spiritual identity. Where a man ceases to sympathise he ceases to live, ceases to see and realise and know.

One cannot truly sympathise with others until all selfish considerations concerning them are put away, and he who does this, and strives to see others as they are, strives to realise their particular sins, temptations, and sorrows, their beliefs, opinions, and prejudices, comes at last to see exactly where they stand in their spiritual evolution, comprehends the arc of their experience, and knows that they cannot for the present act otherwise than they do. He sees that their thoughts and acts are prompted by the extent of their knowledge, or their lack of knowledge, and that if they act blindly and foolishly it is because their knowledge and experience are immature, and they can only come to act more wisely by gradual growth into more enlightened states of mind. He also sees that though this growth can be encouraged, helped, and stimulated by the influence of a riper example, by seasonable words and well-timed instruction, it cannot be unnaturally forced; the flowers of love and wisdom must have time to grow, and the barren branches of hatred and folly cannot be all cut away at once.

Such a man finds the doorway into the inner world of those with whom he comes in contact, and he opens it and enters in and dwells with them in the hidden and sacred sanctuary of their being. And he finds nothing to hate, nothing to revile, nothing to condemn in that sacred place, but something to love and tend, and, in his own heart, room only for greater pity, greater patience, greater love.

He sees that he is one with them, that they are but another aspect of himself, that their natures are not different from his own, except in modification and degree, but are identical with it. If they are acting out certain sinful tendencies he has but to look within to find the same tendencies in himself, albeit, perhaps, restrained or purified; if they are manifesting certain holy and divine qualities he finds the same pure spirit within himself, though, perhaps, in a lesser degree of power and development.

One touch of nature makes the whole world kin.

The sin of one is the sin of all; the virtue of one is the virtue of all. No man can be separate from another. There is no difference of nature but only difference of condition. If a man thinks he is separated from another by virtue of his superior holiness he is not so separated, and his darkness and delusion are very great. Humanity is one, and in the holy sanctuary of sympathy saint and sinner meet and unite.

It is said of Jesus that He took upon Himself the sins of the whole world—that is, He identified Himself with those sins, and did not regard Himself as essentially separate from sinners but as being of a like nature with them—and this realisation of His oneness with all men was manifested in His life as profound sympathy with those who, for their deep sins, were avoided and cast off by others.

And who is it that is in the greatest need of sympathy? Not the saint, not the enlightened seer, not the perfect man. It is the sinner, the unenlightened man, the imperfect one; and the greater the sin the greater is the need. "I came not to call the righteous but sinners to repentance" is the statement of One who comprehended all human needs. The righteous man does not need your sympathy, but the unrighteous; he who, by his wrong-doing, is laying up for himself long periods of suffering and woe is in need of it.

The flagrantly unrighteous man is condemned, despised, and avoided by those who are living in a similar condition to him, though, for the time being, they may not be subject to his particular form of sin, for that withholding of sympathy and that mutual condemnation which are so rife is the commonest manifestation of that lack of understanding in which all sin takes its rise.

While a man is involved in sin he will condemn others who are likewise involved, and the deeper and greater his sin the more severe will be his condemnation of others. It is only when a man begins to sorrow for his sin, and so to rise above it into the clearer light of purity and understanding, that he ceases from condemning others and learns to sympathise with them. But this ceaseless condemnation of each other by those who are involved in the fierce play of the passions must needs be, for it is one of the modes of operation of the Great Law which universally and eternally obtains, and the unrighteous one who falls under the condemnation of his fellows will the more rapidly reach a higher and nobler condition of heart and life if he humbly accepts the censure of others as the effect of his own sin, and resolves henceforward to refrain from all condemnation of others.

The truly good and wise man condemns none; having put away all blind passion and selfishness he lives in the calm regions of love and peace, and understands all modes of sin, with their consequent sufferings and sorrows. Enlightened and awakened, freed from all selfish bias, and seeing men as they are, his heart responds in holy sympathy with all. Should any condemn, abuse, or slander him he throws around them the kindly protection of his sympathy, seeing the ignorance which prompts them so to act, and knowing that they alone will suffer for their wrong acts.

Learn, by self-conquest and the acquisition of wisdom, to love him whom you now condemn, to sympathise with those who condemn you. Turn your eyes away from their condemnation and search your own heart, to find, perchance, some hard, unkind, or wrong thoughts which, when discovered and understood, you will condemn yourself.

Much that is commonly called sympathy is personal affection. To love them who love us is human bias and inclination; but to love them who do not love us is divine sympathy.

Sympathy is needed because of the prevalence of suffering, for there is no being or creature who has not suffered. Through suffering sympathy is evolved. Not in a year or a life or an age is the human heart purified and softened by suffering, but after many lives of intermittent pain, after many ages of ever-recurring sorrow, man reaps the golden harvest of his experiences, and garners in the rich, ripe sheaves of love and wisdom. And then he understands, and, understanding, he sympathises.

All suffering is the result of ignorantly violated law, and after many repetitions of the same wrong act, and the same kind of suffering resulting from that act, knowledge of the law is acquired, and the higher state of obedience and wisdom is reached. Then there blossoms the pure and perfect flower of sympathy.

One aspect of sympathy is that of pity—pity for the distressed or pain-stricken, with a desire to alleviate or help them bear their sufferings. The world needs more of this divine quality.

For pity makes the world
Soft to the weak, and noble for the strong.

But it can only be developed by eradicating all hardness and unkindness, all accusation and resentment. He who, when he sees another suffering for his sin, hardens his heart and thinks or says: "It serves him right"—such a one cannot exercise pity nor apply its healing balm. Every time a man acts cruelly toward another (be it only a dumb creature,) or refuses to bestow needed sympathy, he dwarfs himself, deprives himself of ineffable blessedness, and prepares himself for suffering.

Another form of sympathy is that of rejoicing with those who are more successful than ourselves, as though their success were our own. Blessed indeed is he who is free from all envy and malice, and can rejoice and be glad when he hears of the good fortune of those who regard him as an enemy.

The protecting of creatures weaker and more indefensible than oneself is another form in which this divine sympathy is manifested. The helpless frailty of the dumb creation calls for the exercise of the deepest sympathy. The glory of superior strength resides in its power to shield, not to destroy. Not by the callous destruction of weaker things is life truly lived, but by their preservation:

> *All life*
>
> *Is linked and kin*

and the lowest creature is not separated from the highest but by greater weakness, by lesser intelligence. When we pity and protect we reveal and enlarge the divine life and joy within ourselves. When we thoughtlessly or callously inflict suffering or destroy, then our divine life becomes obscured, and its joy fades and dies. Bodies may feed bodies, and passions passions, but man's divine nature is only nurtured, sustained, and developed by kindness, love, sympathy, and all pure and unselfish acts.

By bestowing sympathy on others we increase our own. Sympathy given can never be wasted. Even the meanest creature will respond to its heavenly touch, for it is the universal language which all creatures understand. I have recently heard a true story of a Dartmoor convict whose terms of incarceration in various convict stations extended to over forty years. As a criminal he was considered one of the most callous and hopelessly abandoned, and the warders found him almost intractable. But one day he caught a mouse—a weak, terrified, hunted thing like himself—and its helpless frailty, and the similarity of its condition with his own, appealed to him, and started into flame the divine spark of sympathy which smouldered in his crime-hardencd heart, and which no human touch had ever wakened into life.

He kept the mouse in an old boot in his cell, fed, tended, and loved it, and in his love for the weak and helpless he forgot and lost his hatred for the strong. His heart and his hand were no longer against his fellows. He became tractable and obedient to the uttermost. The warders could not understand his change; it seemed to them little short of miraculous that this most hardened of all criminals should suddenly become transformed into the likeness of a gentle, obedient child. Even the expression of his features altered remarkably: a pleasing smile began to play around the mouth which had formerly been moved to nothing better than a cruel grin, and the implacable hardness of his eyes disappeared and gave place to a soft, deep mellow light. The criminal was a criminal no longer; he was saved, converted; clothed, and in his right mind; restored to humaneness and to humanity, and set firmly on the pathway to divinity by pitying and caring for a defenceless creature. All this was made known to the warders shortly afterwards, when, on his discharge, he took the mouse away with him.

Thus sympathy bestowed increases its store in our own hearts, and enriches and fructifies our own life. *Sympathy given is blessedness received*; sympathy withheld is blessedness forfeited. In the measure that a man increases and enlarges his sympathy so much nearer does he approach the ideal life, the perfect blessedness; and when his heart has become so mellowed that no hard, bitter, or cruel thought can enter and detract from its permanent sweetness, then indeed is he richly and divinely blessed.

Forgiveness

If men only understood
All the emptiness and aching
Of the sleeping and the waking
Of the souls they judge so blindly,
Of the hearts they pierce unkindly,
They, with gentler words and feeling,
Would apply the balm of healing–
  If they only understood.

Kindness, nobler ever than revenge.
        –Shakespeare

The remembering of injuries is spiritual darkness; the fostering of resentment is spiritual suicide. To resort to the spirit and practice of forgiveness is the beginning of enlightenment; it is also the beginning of peace and happiness. There is no rest for him who broods over slights and injuries and wrongs; no quiet repose of mind for him who feels that he has been unjustly treated, and who schemes how best to act for the discomfiture of his enemy.

How can happiness dwell in a heart that is so disturbed by ill-will? Do birds resort to a burning bush wherein to build and sing? Neither can happiness inhabit in that breast that is aflame with burning thoughts of resentment. Nor can wisdom come and dwell where such folly resides.

Revenge seems sweet only to the mind that is unacquainted with the spirit of forgiveness; but when the sweetness of forgiveness is tasted then the extreme bitterness of revenge is known. Revenge seems to lead to happiness to those who are involved in the darkness of passion; but when the violence of passion is abandoned, and the mildness of forgiveness is resorted to, then it is seen that revenge leads to suffering.

Revenge is a virus which eats into the very vitals of the mind, and poisons the entire spiritual being. Resentment is a mental fever which burns up the wholesome energies of the mind, and "taking offence" is a form of moral sickness which saps the healthy flow of kindliness and good-will, and from which men and women should seek to be delivered. The unforgiving and resentful spirit is a source of great suffering and sorrow, and he who harbors and encourages it, who does not overcome and abandon it, forfeits much blessedness, and does not obtain any measure of true enlightenment. To be hard-hearted is to suffer, is to be deprived of light and comfort; to be tender-hearted is to be serenely glad, is to receive light and be well comforted. It will seem strange to many to be told that the hard-hearted and unforgiving suffer most; yet it is profoundly true, for not only do they, by the law of attraction, draw to themselves the revengeful passions in other people, but their hardness of heart itself is a continual source of suffering. Every time a man hardens his heart against a fellow-being he inflicts upon himself five kinds of suffering—namely, the suffering of loss of love; the suffering of lost communion and fellowship; the suffering of a troubled and confused mind; the suffering of wounded passion or pride; and the suffering of punishment inflicted by others. Every act of unforgiveness entails upon the doer of that act these five sufferings; whereas every act of forgiveness brings to the doer five kinds of blessedness—the blessedness of love; the blessedness of increased communion and fellowship; the blessedness of a calm and peaceful mind; the blessedness of passion stilled and pride overcome; and the blessedness of kindness and good-will bestowed by others.

Numbers of people are Today suffering the fiery torments of an unforgiving spirit, and only when they make an effort to overcome that spirit can they know what a cruel and exacting taskmaster they are serving. Only those who have abandoned the service of such a master for that of the nobler master of forgiveness can realise and know how grievous a service is the one, how sweet the other.

Let a man contemplate the strife of the world: how individuals and communities, neighbors and nations, live in continual retaliations toward each other; let him realise the heartaches, the bitter tears, the grievous partings and misunderstandings—yea, even the bloodshed and woe which spring from that strife—and, thus realising, he will never again yield to ignoble thoughts or resentment, never again take offence at the actions of others, never again live in unforgiveness toward any being.

Have good-will
To all that lives, letting unkindness die,
And greed and wrath; so that your lives be made
Like soft airs passing by.

When a man abandons retaliation for forgiveness he passes from darkness to light. So dark and ignorant is unforgiveness that no being who is at all wise or enlightened could descend to it; but its darkness is not understood and known until it is left behind, and the better and nobler course of conduct is sought and practised. Man is blinded and deluded only by his own dark and sinful tendencies; and the giving up of all unforgiveness means the giving up of pride and certain forms of passion, the abandonment of the deeply-rooted idea of the importance of oneself and of the necessity for protecting and defending that self; and when that is done the higher life, greater wisdom, and pure enlightenment, which pride and passion completely obscured, are revealed in all their light and beauty.

Then there are petty offences, little spites and passing slights, which, while of a less serious nature than deep-seated hatreds and revenges, dwarf the character and cramp the soul. They are due to the sin of self and self-importance, and thrive on vanity. Whosoever is blinded and deluded by vanity will continually see something in the actions and attitudes of others toward him at which to take offence, and the more there is of vanity the more greatly will the imaginary slight or wrong be exaggerated. Moreover, to live in the frequent indulgence of petty resentments increases the spirit of hatred, and leads gradually downward to greater darkness, suffering, and self-delusion.

Don't take offence or allow your feelings to be hurt, which means—get rid of pride and vanity.

Don't give occasion for offence or hurt the feelings of others, which means—be gently considerate, forgiving, and charitable toward all.

The giving up—the total uprooting—of vanity and pride is a great task; but it is a blessed task, and it can be accomplished by constant practice in non-resentment and by meditating upon one's thoughts and actions so as to understand and purify them; and the spirit of forgiveness is perfected in one in the measure that pride and vanity are overcome and abandoned.

The not-taking-offence and the not-giving-offence go together. When a man ceases to resent the actions of others he is already acting kindly toward them, considering them before himself or his own defence. Such a man will be gentle in what he says and does, will arouse love and kindness in others, and not stir them up to ill-will and strife. He will also be free from all fear concerning the actions of others toward him, for he who hurts none fears none. But the unforgiving man, he who is eager to "pay back" some real or imaginary slight or injury, will not be considerate toward others, for he considers himself first, and is continually making enemies; he also lives in the fear of others, thinking that they are trying to do toward him as he is doing toward them. He who contrives the hurt of others fears others.

That is a beautiful story of Prince Dîrghayu which was told by an ancient Indian teacher to his disciples in order to impress them with the truth of the sublime precept that "hatred ceases not by hatred at any time; hatred ceases by not-hatred." The story is as follows:—Brahmadatta, a powerful king of Benares, made war upon Dirgheti, the king of Kosala, in order to annex his kingdom, which was much smaller than his own. Dirgheti, seeing that it was impossible for him to resist the greater power of Brahmadatta, fled, and left his kingdom in his enemy's hand. For some time he wandered from place to place in disguise, and at last settled down with his queen in an artisan's cottage; and the queen gave birth to a son, whom they called Dîrghayu.

Now, King Brahmadatta was anxious to discover the hiding-place of Dirgheti, in order to put to death the conquered king, for he thought, "Seeing that I have deprived him of his kingdom he may some day treacherously kill me if I do not kill him."

But many years passed away, and Dirgheti devoted himself to the education of his son, who, by diligent application became learned and skilful and wise.

And after a time Dîrgheti's secret became known, and he, fearing that Brahmadatta would discover him and slay all three, and thinking more of the life of his son than his own, sent away the prince. Soon after the exile king fell into the hands of Brahmadatta, and was, along with his queen, executed.

Now Brahmadatta thought: "I have got rid of Dirgheti and his queen, but their son, Prince Dîrghayu, lives, and he will be sure to contrive some means of effecting my assassination; yet he is unknown to any, and I have no means of discovering him." So the king lived in great fear and continual distress of mind.

Soon after the execution of his parents, Dîrghayu, under an assumed name, sought employment in the king's stables, and was engaged by the master of the elephants.

Dîrghayu quickly endeared himself to all, and his superior abilities came at last under the notice of the king, who had the young man brought before him, and was so charmed with him that he employed him in his own castle, and he proved to be so able and diligent that the king shortly placed him in a position of great trust under himself.

One day the king went on a long hunting expedition, and became separated from his retinue, Dîrghayu alone remaining with him. And the king, being fatigued with his exertions, lay down, and slept with his head in Dîrghayu's lap.

Then Dîrghayu thought: "This king has greatly wronged me. He robbed my father of his kingdom, and slew my parents, and he is now entirely in my power." And he drew his sword, thinking to slay Brahmadatta. But, remembering how his father had taught him never to seek revenge but to forgive to the uttermost, he sheathed his sword.

At last the king awoke out of a disturbed sleep, and the youth inquired of him why he looked so frightened. "My sleep," said the king, "is always restless, for I frequently dream that I am in the power of young Dîrghayu, and that he is about to slay me. While lying here I again dreamed that dream with greater vividness than ever before, and it has filled me with dread and terror."

Then the youth, drawing his sword, said: "I am Prince Dîrghayu, and you are in my power; the time of vengeance has arrived."

Then the king fell upon his knees and begged Dîrghayu to spare his life. And Dîrghayu said: "It is you, O king! who must spare my life. For many years you have wished to find me in order that you might kill me; and, now that you have found me, let me beg of you to grant to me my life."

And there and then did Brahmadatta and Dîrghayu grant each other life, took hands, solemnly vowed never to harm each other. And so overcome was the king by the noble and forgiving spirit of Dîrghayu that he gave him his daughter in marriage, and restored to him his father's kingdom.

Thus hatred ceases by not-hatred—by forgiveness, which is very beautiful, and is sweeter and more effective than revenge. It is the beginning of love, of that divine love that does not seek its own; and he who practises it, who perfects himself in it, comes at last to realize that blessed state wherein the torments of pride and vanity and hatred and retaliation are for ever dispelled, and good-will and peace are unchanging and unlimited. In that state of calm, silent bliss, even forgiveness passes away, and is no longer needed, for he who has reached it sees no evil to resent but only ignorance and delusion on which to have compassion, and forgiveness is only needed so long as there is any tendency to resent, retaliate, and take offence. Equal love toward all is the perfect law, the perfect life, the perfect state in which all lesser states find their completion. Forgiveness is one of the doorways in the faultless Temple of Divine Love.

Seeing No Evil

The solid, solid universe
Is pervious to Love;
With bandaged eyes he never errs,
Around, below, above,
His blinding light
He flingeth white
On God's and Satan's brood,
And reconciles
By mystic wiles
The evil and the good.

—Emerson

If thou thinkest evil, be thou sure
Thine acts will bear the shadow of the stain;
And if thy thought be perfect, then thy deed
Will be as of the perfect, true and pure.

—After Confucius

After much practice in forgiveness, and having cultivated the spirit of forgiveness up to a certain point, knowledge of the actual nature of good and evil dawns upon the mind, and a man begins to understand how thoughts and motives are formed in the human heart, how they develop, and how take birth in the form of actions. This marks the opening of a new vision in the mind, the commencement of a nobler, higher, diviner life; for the man now begins to perceive that there is no necessity to resist or resent the actions of others toward him, whatever those actions may be, and that all along his resentment has been caused by his own ignorance, and that his own bitterness of spirit is wrong. Having arrived thus far he will tax himself with some such questionings as these: "Why this continual retaliation and forgiveness? Why this tormenting anger against another and then this repentance and forgiveness? Is not forgiveness the taking back of one's anger, the giving up of one's resentment; and if anger and resentment are good and necessary why repent of them and give them up? If it is so beautiful, so sweet, so peaceful to get rid of all feelings of bitterness and utterly and wholly to forgive, would it not be still more beautiful and sweet and peaceful never to grow bitter at all, never to know anger, never to resent as evil the actions of another, but always to live in the experience of that pure, calm, blissful love which is known when an act of forgiveness is done, and all unruly passion toward another is put away? If another has done me wrong is not my hatred toward him wrong, and can one wrong right another? Moreover, has he by his wrong *really* injured me, or has he injured himself? Am I not injured by my own wrong rather than by his? Why, then, do I grow angry? Why do I resent, retaliate, and engage in bitter thoughts? Is it not because my pride is piqued or my vanity wounded or my selfishness thwarted? Is it not because my blind animal passions are aroused and allowed to subdue my better nature? Seeing that I am hurt by another person's attitude toward me because of my own pride or vanity or ungoverned and unpurified passions, would it not be better to look to the wrong in myself rather than the wrong in another, to get rid of pride and vanity and passion, and so avoid being hurt at all?"

By such self-questionings and their elucidation in the light of mild thoughts and dispassionate conduct a man, gradually overcoming passion and rising out of the ignorance which gave rise to passion, will at last reach that blessed state in which he will cease to see evil in others, and will dwell in universal good-will and love and peace. Not that he will cease to see ignorance and folly; not that he will cease to see suffering and sorrow and misery; not that he will cease to distinguish between acts that are pure and impure, right and wrong, for, having put away passion and prejudice, he will see these things in the full, clear light of knowledge, and exactly as they are; but he will cease to see anything—any evil power—in another which can do him injury, which he must violently oppose and strive to crush, and against which he must guard himself. Having arrived at a right understanding of evil by purging it away from his own heart he sees that it is a thing that does not call for hatred and fear and resentment but for consideration, compassion, and love.

Shakespeare through one of his characters says: "There is no darkness but ignorance." All evil is ignorance, is dense darkness of mind, and the removal of sin from one's mind is a coming out of darkness into spiritual light. Evil is the negation of good, just as darkness is the negation, or absence, of light, and what is there in a negation to arouse anger or resentment? When night settles down upon the world who is so foolish as to rail at the darkness? The enlightened man, likewise, does not accuse or condemn the spiritual darkness in men's hearts which is manifested in the form of sin, though by gentle reproof he may sometimes point out where the light lies.

Now the ignorance to which I refer as evil, or as the source of evil, is two-fold. There is wrong-doing which is committed without any knowledge of good and evil, and where there is no choice—this is unconscious wrong-doing. Then there is wrong-doing which is done in the knowledge that it ought not to be done—this is conscious wrong-doing; but both unconscious and conscious wrong-doing arise in ignorance—that is, *ignorance of the real nature and painful consequences of the wrong-doing.*

Why does a man continue to do certain things which he feels he ought not to do? If he knows that what he is doing is wrong where lies the ignorance?

He continues to do those things because his knowledge of them is incomplete. He only knows he ought not to do them by certain precepts without and qualms of conscience within, but he does not fully and completely understand what he is doing. He knows that certain acts bring him immediate pleasure, and so, in spite of the troubled conscience which follows that pleasure, he continues to commit them. He is convinced that the pleasure is good and desirable, and therefore to be enjoyed. He does not know that pleasure and pain are one, but thinks he can have the one without the other. He has no knowledge of the law which governs human actions, and never thinks of associating his sufferings with his own wrong-doing, but believes that they are caused by the wrong-doing of others or are the mysterious dispensations of Providence, and therefore not to be inquired into or understood. He is seeking happiness, and does those things which he believes will bring him most enjoyment, but he acts in entire ignorance of the hidden and inevitable consequences which attach to his actions.

Said a man to me once who was the victim of a bad habit: "I know the habit is a bad one, and that it does me more harm than good." I said: "If you *know* that what you are doing is bad and harmful why do you continue to do it?" And he replied: "Because it is pleasant, and I like it."

This man, of course, did not really *know* that his habit was bad. He had been told that it was, and he thought he knew or believed it was, but in reality he thought it was good, that it was conducive to his happiness and well-being, and therefore he continued to practice it. When a man knows by experience that a thing is bad, and that every time he does it he injures body or mind, or both; when his knowledge of that thing is so complete that he is acquainted with its whole train of baneful effects, then he cannot only not do it any longer, he cannot even desire to do it, and even the pleasure that was formerly in that thing becomes painful. No man would put a venomous snake in his pocket because it was prettily coloured. Man knows that a deadly sting lurks in those beautiful markings. Nor, when a man knows the unavoidable pain and hurt which lie hidden in wrong thoughts and acts, does he continue to think and commit them. Even the immediate pleasure which formerly he greedily sought is gone from them; their surface attractiveness has vanished; he is no longer ignorant concerning their true nature; he sees them as they are.

I knew a young man who was in business, and, although a member of a church, and occupying the position of a voluntary religious instructor, he told me that it was absolutely necessary to practice lying and deception in business, otherwise sure and certain ruin would follow. He said he *knew* lying was wrong, but while he remained in business he must continue to do it. Upon questioning him I found, of course, that he had never tried truth and honesty in his business, had not even thought of trying the better way, so firmly convinced was he that it was not a "better way," so that it was not possible for him to know whether or not it would be productive of ruin. Now did this young man *know* that lying was wrong? There was a preceptial sense only in which he knew, but there was a deeper and more real sense in which he did not know. He had been taught to regard lying as wrong, and his conscience bore out that teaching, but he believed that it brought to him profit, prosperity, and happiness, and that honesty would bring him loss, poverty, and misery—in a word, he regarded lying, deep in his heart, as the right thing to do, and honesty as the wrong practice. He had no knowledge whatever of the real nature of the act of lying: how it *is*, on the instant of its committal, loss of character, loss of self-respect, loss of power, usefulness, and influence, and loss of blessedness; and how it unerringly leads to loss of reputation and loss of material profit and prosperity. Only when such a man begins to consider the happiness of others, and prefers to embrace the loss which he fears rather than clutch at the gain which he desires, will he obtain that real knowledge which lofty moral conduct alone can reveal; and then, experiencing the greater blessedness, he will see how, all along, he has been deceiving and defrauding himself rather than others, has been living in darkest ignorance and self-delusion.

These two common instances of wrong-doing will serve to illustrate and make plainer, to those of my readers who, while searching for Truth, are as yet doubtful, uncertain, and confused, the deep Truth that all sin, or evil, is a condition of ignorance, and therefore to be dealt with in a loving and not a hateful spirit.

And as with bad habits and lying so with all sin—with lust, hatred, malice, envy, pride, vanity, self-indulgence, and selfishness in all its forms: it is a state of spiritual darkness, the absence of the Light of Truth in the heart, the negation of knowledge.

Thus when, by overcoming the wrong condition in one's own heart, the nature of evil is fully realised, and mere belief gives place to living knowledge, evil can no longer be hatefully condemned and violently resisted, and the wrong-doer is thought of with tender compassion.

And this brings us to another aspect of evil—namely, that of individual freedom; the right of every person to choose his own actions. Along with the seeing of evil in others is the desire to convert or coerce others into one's own ways of thinking and acting. Probably the commonest delusion in which men are involved is that of thinking that what they themselves believe and think and do is good, and all that is otherwise is evil, and therefore to be powerfully condemned and resisted. It is out of this delusion that all persecution springs. There are Christians who regard all Atheists as men wholly evil, as given up to the service of an evil power; and there are Atheists who firmly believe that all Christians are doing the greatest harm to the whole human race by their "superstitious and false doctrines." The truth is that neither the Christian nor the Atheist is evil, nor in the service of evil, but each is choosing his own way, and is pursuing that course which he is convinced is right.

Let a man quietly contemplate the fact that numbers of followers of various religions the world over are, as they ever were, engaged in condemning each other as evil and wrong, and regarding themselves as good and right, and it will help him to realise how all evil is merely ignorance, spiritual darkness; and earnest meditation on that fact will be found to be one of the greatest aids in developing greater kindness, charity, insight, and breadth of mind.

The truly wise and good man sees good in all, evil in none. He has abandoned the folly of wanting others to think and act as he thinks and acts, for he sees that men are variously constituted, are at different points in their spiritual evolution, and must, of necessity, think and act differently. Having put away hatred, condemnation, egotism, and prejudice he has become enlightened, and sees that purity, love, compassion, gentleness, patience, humility, and unselfishness are manifestations of light and knowledge; while impurity, hatred, cruelty, passion, anger, pride, and selfishness are manifestations of darkness and ignorance; and that whether men are living in light or darkness they are one and all doing that which they think is necessary, are acting in accordance with their own measure of light or darkness. The wise man understands, and, understanding, he ceases from all bitterness and accusation.

Every man acts in accordance with his nature, with his own sense of right and wrong, and is surely gathering in the results of his own experience. There is one supreme right which every being possesses—the right to think and act as he chooses. If he chooses to think and act selfishly, thinking of his own immediate happiness only and not of that of others, then he will rapidly bring upon himself, by the action of the moral law of cause and effect, such afflictions as will cause him to pause and consider, and so find a better way. There is no teacher to compare with experience, no chastisement so corrective and purifying as that which men ignorantly inflict upon themselves. The selfish man is the ignorant man; he chooses his own way, but it is a way which leads to suffering, and through suffering to knowledge and bliss. The good man is the wise man: he likewise chooses his own way, but he chooses it in the full light of knowledge, having passed through the stages of ignorance and suffering, and arrived at knowledge and bliss.

A man begins to understand what "seeing no evil" is when, putting away all personal desires in his judgments of others, he considers them from their own standpoint, and judges their actions not from his own standard *but from theirs*. It is because men set up arbitrary standards of right and wrong, and are anxious that all should conform to their particular standard, that they see evil in each other. A man is only rightly judged when he is judged not from my standard or yours but from his own, and to deal with him thus is not judgment—it is Love. It is only when we look through the eyes of Impersonal Love that we become enlightened, and see others as they really are; and a man is approaching that Love when he can say in his heart: "Who am I that I should judge another? Am I so pure and sinless that I arraign men and pass the judgment of evil upon them? Rather let me humble myself, and correct mine own errors, before assuming the position of supreme judge of those of other men."

It was said by one of old to those who were about to stone, as evil, a woman taken in the act of committing one of the darkest of sins: "He that is without sin let him cast the first stone;" and though he who said it was without sin yet he took up no stone, nor passed any bitter judgment, but said, with Infinite gentleness and compassion: "Neither do I condemn thee; go, and sin no more."

In the pure heart there is no room left where personal judgments and hatreds can find lodgment, for it is filled to overflowing with tenderness and love: it sees no evil; and only as men succeed in seeing no evil in others will they become free from sin and sorrow and suffering.

No man sees evil in himself or his own acts except the man who is becoming enlightened, and then he abandons those acts which he has come to see are wrong. Every man justifies himself in what he does, and, however evil others may regard his conduct, he himself thinks it to be good and necessary; if he did not he would not, could not, do it. The angry man always justifies his anger; the covetous man his greed; the impure man his unchastity; the liar considers that his lying is altogether necessary; the slanderer believes that, in vilifying the characters of those whom he dislikes, and warning other people against their "evil" natures, he is doing well; the thief is convinced that stealing is the shortest and best way to plenty, prosperity, and happiness; and even the murderer thinks that there is a ground of justification for his deed.

Every man's deeds are in accordance with the measure of his own light or darkness, and no man can live higher than he is or act beyond the limits of his knowledge. Nevertheless, he can improve himself, and thereby gradually increase his light and extend the range of his knowledge. The angry man indulges in raillery and abuse because his knowledge does not extend to forbearance and patience. Not having practised gentleness he does not understand it, and cannot choose it; nor can he know, by its comparison with the light of gentleness, the darkness of anger. It is the same with the liar, the slanderer, and the thief: he lives in this dark condition of mind and action because he is limited to it by his immature knowledge and experience, because, never having lived in the higher conditions, he has no knowledge of them, and it is, to him, as if they were non-existent: "The light shineth in the darkness, and the darkness comprehendeth it not." Nor can he understand even the conditions in which he is living, because, being dark, they are necessarily devoid of all knowledge.

When a man, driven by repeated sufferings at last to reflect upon his conduct, comes to see that his anger or lying, or whatever ignorant condition he may have been living in, is productive only of trouble and sorrow, then he abandons it, and begins to search for, and practice, the opposite and enlightened condition; and when he is firmly established in the better way, so that his knowledge of both conditions is complete, then he realises in what great darkness he had formerly lived.

This knowledge of good and evil by experience constitutes enlightenment.

When a man begins to look, as it were, through the eyes of others, and to measure them by their own standard and not by his, then he ceases from the seeing of evil in others, for he knows that every man's perception and standard of good and evil is different; that there is no vice so low but some men regard it as good; no virtue so high but some men regard it as evil; and what a man regards as good that to him is good; what he regards as evil that to him is evil.

Nor will the purified man, who has ceased to see evil in others, have any desire to win men to his own ways or opinions, but will rather help them in their own particular groove, knowing that an enlarged experience only, and not merely change of opinion, can lead to higher knowledge and greater blessedness.

It will be found that men see evil in those who differ from them, good in those who agree with them. The man who greatly loves himself and is enamored of his opinions will love all those who agree with him and will dislike all those who disagree with him. "If ye love them that love ye, what reward have ye? . . . Love your enemies, do good to them that hate you." Egotism and vanity make men blind. Men of opposing religious views hate and per-

secute each other; men of opposing political views
fight and condemn each other. The partisan measures all men by his own standard, and sets up his
judgments accordingly. So convinced is he that he
is right and others wrong that he at last persuades
himself that to inflict cruelty on others is both good
and necessary in order to coerce them into his way
of thinking and acting, and so bring them to the
right—his right—against their own reason and will.

Men hate, condemn, resist, and inflict suffering
upon each other, not because they are intrinsically
evil, not because they are deliberately "wicked,"
and are doing, in the full light of truth, what they
know to be wrong, but because they regard such
conduct as necessary and right. All men are intrinsically good, but some are wiser than others, are
older in experience than others.

I recently heard, in substance, the following
conversation between two men whom I will call
D_____ and E_____. The third person referred to
as X_____ is a prominent politician:

- E. Every man reaps the result of his own thoughts
  and deeds, and suffers for his own wrong.
- D. If that is so, and if no man can escape from
  the penalty of his evil deeds, what an inferno
  some of our men in power must be preparing
  for themselves.

E. Whether a man is in power or not, so long as he lives in ignorance and sin, he will reap sorrow and suffering.

D. Look, for instance, at X_____, a man totally evil, given up entirely to selfishness and ambition; surely great torments are reserved for so unprincipled a man.

E. But how do you know he is so evil?

D. By his works, his fruits. When I see a man doing evil I know that he is evil; and I cannot even think of X_____ but I burn with righteous indignation. I am sometimes inclined to doubt that there is an overruling power for good when I see such a man in a position where he can do so much harm to others.

E. What evil is he committing?

D. His whole policy is evil. He will ruin the country if he remains in power.

E. But, while there are large numbers of people who think of X_____ as you do, there are also large numbers, equally intelligent, who look upon him as good and able, who admire him for his excellent qualities, and regard his policy as beneficent and making for national progress.

   He owes his position to these people, are they also evil?

D. They are deceived and misled. And this only makes X_____'s evil all the greater, in that he can so successfully employ his talents in deceiving others in order to gain his own selfish ends. I hate the man.

E. May it not be possible that you are deceived?

D. In what way?

E. Hatred is self-deception; love is self-enlightenment. No man can see either himself or others clearly until he ceases from hatred and practises love.

D. That sounds very beautiful, but it is impracticable. When I see a man doing evil to others, and deceiving and misleading them, I *must* hate him. It is right that I should do so. X_____ is without a spark of conscience.

E. X_____ may or may not be all you believe him to be, but, even if he is, according to your own words, he should be pitied and not condemned.

D. How so?

E. You say he is without a conscience.

D. Entirely so.

E. Then he is a mental cripple. Do you hate the blind because they cannot see, the dumb because they cannot speak, or the deaf because they cannot hear? When a captain has lost his rudder or broken his compass do you condemn him because he did not keep his ship off the rocks?

Do you hold him responsible for the loss of life?

If a man is totally devoid of conscience he is without the means of moral guidance, and all his selfishness must, perforce, appear to him good and right and proper. X_____ may appear evil to you, but is he evil to himself? Does he regard his own conduct as evil?

D. Whether he regards himself as evil or not he is evil.

E. If I were to regard you as evil because of your hatred for X_____, should I be right?

D. No.

E. Why not?

D. Because in such a case hatred is necessary, justifiable, and righteous. There is such a thing as righteous anger, righteous hatred.

E. Is there such a thing as righteous selfishness, righteous ambition, righteous evil? I should be quite wrong in regarding you as evil, because you are doing what you are convinced is right, because you regard your hatred for X_____ as part of your duty as a man and a citizen; nevertheless, there is a better way than that of hatred, and it is the knowledge of this better way that prevents me from hating X_____ as you do, because, however wrong his conduct might appear to me, it is not wrong to him, nor to his supporters; moreover, all men reap as they sow.

D. What, then, is that better way?

E. It is the way of Love; the ceasing to regard others as evil. It is a blessed and peaceful state of heart.

D. Do you mean that there is a state which a man can reach wherein he will not grow angry when he sees people doing evil?

E. No, I do not mean that, for while a man regards others as evil he will continue to grow angry with them; but I mean that a man can reach a state of calm insight and spotless love wherein he sees no evil to grow angry with, wherein he understands the various natures of men—how they are prompted to act, and how they reap, as the harvest of their own thoughts and deeds, the tares of suffering and the corn of bliss. To reach that state is to regard all men with compassion and love.

D. The state that you picture is a very high one—it is, no doubt, a very holy and beautiful one—but it is a state that I should be sorry to reach; and I should pray to be preserved from a state of mind wherein I could not hate a man like X____ with an intense hatred.

Thus by this conversation it will be seen that D_____ regarded his hatred as good. Even so all men regard that which they do as necessary to be done. The things which men habitually practice those things they believe in. When faith in a thing wholly ceases it ceases to be practised. D_____'s individual liberty is equal to that of other men, and he has a right to hate another if he so wishes; nor will he abandon his hatred until he discovers, by the sorrow and unrest which it entails, how wrong and foolish and blind it is, and how, by its practice, he is injuring himself.

A great Teacher was once asked by one of His disciples to explain the distinction between good and evil, and, holding His hand with the fingers pointing downward, He said: "Where is my hand pointing?"

And the disciple replied: "It is pointing downward."

Then, turning His hand upward, the Teacher asked: "Where now is my hand pointing?"

And the disciple answered: "It is pointing upward."

"That," said the Teacher, "is the distinction between evil and good."

By this simple illustration He indicated that evil is merely wrongly-directed energy, and good rightly-directed energy, and that the so-called evil man becomes good by reversing his conduct.

To understand the true nature of evil by living in the good is to cease to see other men as evil. Blessed is he who, turning from the evil in others, exerts himself in the purification of his own heart. He shall one day become of "too pure eyes to behold evil."

Knowing the nature of evil, what does it behoove a man to do? It behooves him to live only in that which is good; therefore, if a man condemn me, I will not condemn him in return; if he revile me I will give him kindness; if he slander me I will speak of his good qualities; if he hate me then he greatly needs, and shall receive, my love. With the impatient I will be patient; with the greedy I will be generous; and with the violent and quarrelsome I will be mild and peaceable. Seeing no evil, whom should I hate, or who regard as mine enemy?

Were mankind murderous or jealous upon you,
my brother, my sister?
I'm so sorry for you. They are not murderous or
jealous upon me;
All has been gentle with me, I keep no account
with lamentation;
What have I to do with lamentation?

He who sees men as evil imagines that behind those acts which are called "wicked" there is a corporate and substantial evil prompting those particular sins, but he of stainless vision sees the deeds themselves as the evil, and knows that there is no evil power, no evil soul or man behind those deeds. The substance of the universe is good; there is no substance of evil. Good alone is permanent; there is no fixed or permanent evil.

As brothers and sisters, born of the same parents and being of one household, love each other through all vicissitudes, see no evil in each other, but overlook all errors, and cling together in the strong bonds of affection—even so the good man sees humanity as one spiritual family, born of the same Father-Mother, being of the same essence and making for the same goal, and he regards all men and women as his brothers and sisters, makes no divisions and distinctions, sees none as evil, but is at peace with all. Happy is he who attains to this blessed state.

Abiding Joy

Who carry music in their heart
Through dusky lane and wrangling mart,
Plying their daily toil with busier feet,
Because their secret souls a holier strain
    repeat.

–Keble

Serene will be our days and bright,
    And happy will our nature be,
When love is an unerring light,
    And joy its own security.

–Wordsworth

Abiding joy! Is there such a thing? Where is it? Who possesses it? Yea; there is such a thing. It is where there is no sin. It is possessed by the pure-hearted.

As darkness is a passing shadow, and light is substance that remains, so sorrow is fleeting, but joy abides forever. No true thing can pass away and become lost; no false thing can remain and be preserved. Sorrow is false, and it cannot live; joy is true, and it cannot die. Joy may become hidden for a time, but it can always be recovered; sorrow may remain for a period, but it can be transcended and dispersed.

Do not think your sorrow will remain; it will pass away like a cloud. Do not believe that the torments of sin are ever your portion; they will vanish like a hideous nightmare. Awake! arise! Be holy and joyful!

You are the creator of your own shadows; you desire and then you grieve; renounce, and then you shall rejoice.

You are not the impotent slave of sorrow; the Never-Ending Gladness awaits your Home-coming. You are not the helpless prisoner of the darkness and dreams of sin; even now the beautiful light of holiness shines upon your sleeping lids, ready to greet your awakening vision.

In the heavy, troubled sleep of sin and self the abiding joy is lost and forgotten; its undying music is no more heard and the fragrance of its fadeless flowers no longer cheers the heart of the wayfarer.

But when sin and self are abandoned, when the clinging to things for personal pleasure is put away, then the shadows of grief disappear, and the heart is restored to its Imperishable Joy.

Joy comes and fills the self-emptied heart; it abides with the peaceful; its reign is with the pure.

Joy flees from the selfish; it deserts the quarrelsome; it is hidden from the impure.

Joy is as an angel so beautiful and delicate and chaste that she can only dwell with holiness. She cannot remain with selfishness; she is wedded to Love.

Joy is revealed just in the measure that selfish desire is put away, and although the full, living consciousness of its abidingness, the unbroken continuance of its presence from moment to moment, is reserved only for the altogether pure, its sweetness is tasted by all in their moments or hours of unselfish exaltation. In every truly unselfish thought and act the joy which is not excitement, not that feverish thing called pleasure, and which is followed by no tearful reaction, is revealed.

Every man is truly happy in so far as he is unselfish; he is miserable in so far as he is selfish. All truly good men, and by good men I mean those who have fought victoriously the battle against self, are men of joy. How great is the jubilation of the saint! No true teacher promises sorrow as the ultimate of life; he promises joy. He points to sorrow, but only as a *process* which sin has rendered necessary. Where self ends grief passes away. Joy is the companion of righteousness. In the divine life tender compassion fills the place where weeping sorrow sat. During the process of *becoming* unselfish there are periods of deep sorrow. Purification is necessarily severe. All becoming is painful. Abiding joy in its completion is realised only in the perfection of being, and this is

> *A state*
> *Where all is loveliness, and power and love,*
> *With all sublimest qualities of mind,*
> *. . . Where all*
> *Enjoy entire dominion o'er themselves,*
> *Acts, feelings, thoughts conditions qualities.*

Consider how a flower evolves and becomes: at first there is a little germ groping its way in the dark soil toward the upper light; then the plant appears, and leaf is added unto leaf; and finally the perfected flower appears, in the sweet perfume and chaste beauty of which all effort ceases.

So with human life: at first the blind groping for the light in the dark soil of selfishness and ignorance; then the coming into the light, and the gradual overcoming of selfishness with its accompanying pain and sorrow; and finally the perfect flower of a pure, unselfish life, giving forth, without effort, the perfume of holiness and the beauty of joy.

The good, the pure, are the superlatively happy. However men may argumentatively deny or qualify this, humanity instinctively knows it to be true. Do not men everywhere picture their angels as the most joyful of beings? There are joyful angels in bodies of flesh; we meet them and pass on; and how many of those who come in contact with them are sufficiently pure to see the vision within the form—to see the incorruptible angel in its common instrument of clay?

They needs must grope who cannot see,
The blade before the ear must be;
The outward symbols disappear
From him whose inward sight is clear.

Yes; the pure are the joyful. We look almost in vain for any expressions of sorrow in the words of Jesus. The "Man of Sorrows" is only completed in the Man of Joy.

I Buddha, who wept with all my brothers' tears,
    Whose heart was broken by a whole world's
    woe,
Laugh and am glad, for there is Liberty!

In sin, and in the struggle against sin, there is unrest and affliction, but in the perfection of Truth, in the Path of Righteousness, there is abiding joy.

Enter the Path! There spring the healing streams
    Quenching all thirst! There bloom th' immortal
    flowers
Carpeting all the way with joy! There throng
    Swiftest and sweetest hours!

Tribulation lasts only so long as there remains some chaff of self which needs to be removed. The *tribulum,* or threshing-machine, ceases to work when all the grain is separated from the chaff; and when the last impurities are blown away from the soul tribulation has completed its work, and there is no more need for it; then abiding joy is realised.

All the saints and prophets and saviours of the race have proclaimed with rejoicing the "Gospel," or the "Good News." All men know what good news is—an impending calamity avoided, a disease cured, friends arrived or returned in safety, difficulties overcome, success in some enterprise assured—but what is the "Good News" of the saintly ones? This: that there is peace for the troubled, healing for the afflicted, gladness for the grief-stricken, victory for the sinful, a home-coming for the wanderer, and joy for the sorrowing and broken-hearted. Not that these beautiful realities *shall be* in some future world, but that they are here and now, that they are known and realised and enjoyed; and are, therefore, proclaimed that all may accept them who will break the galling bonds of self and rise into the glorious liberty of unselfish love.

Seek the highest Good, and as you find it, as you practice it and realise it, you will taste the deepest, sweetest joy. As you succeed in forgetting your own selfish desires in your thoughtfulness for others, in your care and love for others, in your service for others, just so far and no further will you find and realise the abiding joy in life.

Inside the gateway of unselfishness lies the elysium of Abiding Joy, and whosoever will may enter in, whosoever doubts let him come and see.

And knowing this—that selfishness leads to misery, and unselfishness to joy, not merely for one's self alone—for if this were all how unworthy would be our endeavors!—but for the whole world, and because all with whom we live and come in contact will be the happier and the truer for our unselfishness; because Humanity is one, and the joy of one is the joy of all—knowing this, let us scatter flowers and not thorns in the common ways of life—yea, even in the highway of our enemies let us scatter the blossoms of unselfish love—so shall the pressure in their footprints fill the air with the perfume of holiness and gladden the world with the aroma of joy.

Silentness

Be still! The crown of life is silentness.
    Give thou a quiet hour to each long day,
Too much of time we spend in profitless
    And foolish talk. Too little do we say.

If thou wouldst gather words that shall avail,
    Learning a wisdom worthy to express,
Leave for a while thy chat and empty tale—
    Study the golden speech of silentness.

–A. L. Salmon

Be still, my soul.
Rest awhile from the feverish activities in
    which you lose yourself.
Be not afraid to be left alone with yourself for
    one short hour.

–Ernest Crosby

In the words of a wise man there is great power, but his silence is more powerful still. The greatest men teach us most effectively when they are purposely silent. The silent attitude of the great man, noted, perhaps, by one or two of his disciples only, is recorded and preserved through the ages; while the obtrusive words of the merely clever talker, heard, perhaps, by thousands, and at once popularised, are neglected and forgotten in, at most, a few generations. The silence of Jesus, when asked by Pilate "What is Truth?" is the impressive, the awful silence of profound wisdom; it is pregnant with humility and reproof, and perpetually rebukes that shallowness that, illustrating the truth that "fools step in where angels fear to tread," would in terms of triteness parcel out the universe, or think to utter the be-all and the end-all of the mystery of things in some textual formula or theological platitude. When, plied with questions about Brahma (God) by the argumentative Brahmans, Buddha remained silent, he taught them better than they knew, and if by his silence he failed to satisfy the foolish he thereby profoundly instructed the wise. Why all this ceaseless talk about God, with its accompaniment of intolerance? Let men practice some measure of kindliness and good-will, and thereby acquaint themselves with the simple rudiments of wisdom. Why all these speculative arguments about the nature of God? Let us first understand somewhat of ourselves. There are no greater marks of folly and moral immaturity than irreverence and presumption; no greater manifestations of wisdom and moral maturity than reverence and humility. Lao-Tze, in his own life, exemplified his teaching that the wise man "teaches without words." Disciples were attracted to him by the power which ever accompanies a wise reserve. Living in comparative obscurity and silence, not courting the ear of men, and never going out to teach, men sought him out and learned of him wisdom.

The silent acts of the Great Ones are beacons to the wise, illuminating their pathway with no uncertain radiance, for he who would attain to virtue and wisdom must learn, not only when to speak and what to say, but also when to remain silent and what not to say. The right control of the tongue is the beginning of wisdom; the right control of the mind is the consummation of wisdom. By curbing his tongue a man gains possession of his mind, and to have complete possession of one's mind is to be a Master of Silence.

The fool babbles, gossips, argues, and bandies words. He glories in the fact that he has had the last word and has silenced his opponent. He exults in his own folly, is ever on the defensive, and wastes his energies in unprofitable channels. He is like a gardener who continues to dig and plant in unproductive soil.

The wise man avoids idle words, gossip, vain argument, and self-defence. He is content to appear defeated; rejoices when he *is* defeated, knowing that, having found and removed another error in himself, he has thereby become wiser. Blessed is he who does not strive for the last word!

> *Backward I see in my own days where I sweated through fog with linguists and contenders;*
> *I have no mockings or arguments, I witness and wait.*

Silence under provocation is the mark of a cultured and sympathetic soul. The thoughtless and unkind are stirred by every slight provocation, and will lose their mental balance by even the appearance of a personal encroachment. The self-possession of Jesus is not a miracle; it is the flower of culture, the diadem of wisdom. When we read of Jesus that "He answered never a word," and of Buddha that "He remained silent," we get a glimpse of the vast power of silence, of the silent majesty of true greatness.

The silent man is the powerful man. The victim of garrulity is devoid of influence; his spiritual energies are dissipated. Every mechanic knows that before a force can be utilised and definitely directed it must be conserved and stored; and the wise man is a spiritual mechanic who conserves the energies of his mind, holds them in masterful abeyance, ready at any moment to direct them, with effective purpose, to the accomplishment of some necessary work.

The true strength is in silentness. It is well said that "The dog that barks does not bite." The grim and rarely broken silence of the bull-dog is the necessary adjunct to that powerfully concentrated and effectual action for which the animal is known and feared. This, of course, is a lower form of silentness, but the principle is the same. The boaster fails; his mind is diverted from the main purpose; and his energies are frittered away upon self-glorification. His forces are divided between his task and the reward to himself, the greater portion going to feed the lust of reward. He is like an unskilful general who loses the battle through dividing his forces instead of concentrating them upon a point. Or he is like a careless engineer who leaves open the waste-valve of his engine and allows the steam to run down. The modest, silent, earnest man succeeds: freed from vanity, and avoiding the dissipation of self-glorification, all his powers are concentrated upon the successful performance of his task. Even while the other man is talking about his powers he is already about his work, and is so much nearer than the other to its completion. It is a law everywhere and always that energy distributed is subject unto energy conserved. The noisy and boasting Charles will ever be thrown by the quiet and modest Orlando.

It is a law universally applicable that quietness is strength. The business man who succeeds never talks about his plans, methods and affairs, and should he, turned giddy by success, begin to do this he will then commence to fail. The man of great moral influence never talks about himself and his spiritual victories, for, should he do so, in that moment his moral power and influence would be gone, and, like Samson, he would be shorn of his strength. Success, worldly or spiritual, is the willing servant of strong, steady, silent, unflinching purpose. The most powerful disintegrating forces make no noise. The greatly-overcoming mind works silently.

If you would be strong, useful, and self-reliant learn the value and power of silentness. Do not talk about yourself. The world instinctively knows that the vain talker is weak and empty, and so it leaves him to his own vanity. Do not talk about what you are going to do but do it, and let your finished work speak for itself. Do not waste your forces in criticising and disparaging the work of others but set about to do your own work thoroughly and well. The worst work with earnestness and sweetness behind it is altogether better than barking at others. While you are disparaging the work of others you are neglecting your own. If others are doing badly help and instruct them by doing better yourself. Neither abuse others nor account their abuse of any weight. When attacked remain silent; in this way you will conquer yourself, and will, without the use of words, teach others.

But the true silence is not merely a silent tongue; it is a *silent mind*. To merely hold one's tongue, and yet to carry about a disturbed and rankling mind, is no remedy for weakness and no source of power. Silentness, to be powerful, must envelop the whole mind, must permeate every chamber of the heart; it must be the silence of peace. To this broad, deep, abiding silentness a man attains only in the measure that he conquers himself. While passions, temptations, and sorrows disturb, the holier, profounder depths of silence are yet to be sounded. To smart under the words and actions of others means that you are yet weak, uncontrolled, unpurified. So rid your heart of the disturbing influences of vanity and pride and selfishness that no petty spite can reach you, no slander or abuse disturb your serene repose. As the storm rages ineffectually against a well-built house, while its occupant sits composed and happy by his fireside within, so no evil without can disturb or harm him who is well fortified with wisdom; self-governed and silent, he remains at peace within. To this great silence the self-conquered man attains.

Envy and calumny, and hate and pain,
And that unrest which men miscall delight,
Can touch him not, nor torture him again.

There is no commoner error amongst men than that of supposing that nothing can be accomplished without much talking and much noise The busy, shallow talker regards the quiet thinker or silent doer as a man wasted; he thinks silentness means "doing nothing," and that hurrying, bustling, and ceaseless talking means "doing much." He also confounds popularity with power. But the thinker and doer is the real and effectual worker. His work is at the root and core and substance of things, and as Nature silently, yet with hidden and wondrous alchemy, transmutes the rude elements of earth and air into tender leaves, beautiful flowers, delectable fruits,—yea, into a myriad forms of beauty—even so does the silent, purposeful worker transform the ways of men and the face of the world by the might and magic of his silently-directed energy. He wastes no time and force in tinkering with the everchanging and artificial surface of things, but goes to the living vital centre, and works therefrom and thereon; and in due season, perhaps when his perishable form is withdrawn from the world, the fruits of his obscure but imperishable labors come forth to gladden the world. But the words of the talker perish. The world reaps no harvest from the sowing of sound.

He who conserves his mental forces also conserves his physical forces. The strongly quiet, calm man lives to a greater age, and in the possession of better health, than the hurrying, noisy man. Quiet, subdued mental harmony is conducive to physical harmony—health. The followers of George Fox are today the healthiest, longest-lived, and most successful portion of the British community, and they live quiet, unostentatious, purposeful lives, avoiding all worldly excitements and unnecessary words. They are a silent people, all their meetings being conducted on the principle that "silence is power."

Silentness is powerful because it is the outcome of self-conquest, and the more successfully a man governs himself the more silent be becomes. As he succeeds in living to a purpose and not to the plea-

sures of self he withdraws himself from the outer
discords of the world and reaches to the inward
music of peace. Then when he speaks there is purpose and power behind his words, and when he
maintains silence there is equal or even greater
power therein. He does not utter that which is followed by pain and tears; does not do that which
is productive of sorrow and remorse. But, saying
and doing those things only which are ripe with
thoughtfulness, his conscience is quiet, and all his
days are blessed.

Why idly seek from outward things
The answer inward silence brings?
Why climb the far-off hills with pain,
A nearer view of heaven to gain?
In lowliest depths of bosky dells
The hermit Contemplation dwells,
Whence, piercing heaven, with screened sight,
He sees at noon the stars, whose light
Shall glorify the coming night.
                                        —Whittier

In the still hour when passion is at rest,
Gather up stores of wisdom in thy breast.
                                        —Wordsworth

Solitude

Man's essential being is inward, invisible, spiritual, and as such it derives its life, its strength, from within, not from without. Outward things are channels through which its energies are expended, but for renewal it must fall back on the inward silence. In so far as man strives to drown this silence in the noisy pleasures of the senses, and endeavors to live in the conflicts of outward things, just so much does he reap the experiences of pain and sorrow, which, becoming at last intolerable, drive him back to the feet of the inward Comforter, to the shrine of the peaceful solitude within.

As the body cannot thrive on empty husks, neither can the spirit be sustained on empty pleasures. If not regularly fed the body loses its vitality, and, pained with hunger and thirst, cries out for food and drink. It is the same with the spirit: it must be regularly nourished in solitude on pure and holy thoughts or it will lose its freshness and strength, and will at last cry out in its painful and utter starvation. The yearning of an anguish-stricken soul for light and consolation is the cry of a spirit that is perishing of hunger and thirst. All pain and sorrow is spiritual starvation, and aspiration is the cry for food. It is the Prodigal Son who, perishing of hunger, turns his face longingly toward his Father's home.

The pure life of the spirit cannot be found, but is lost, in the life of the senses. The lower desires are ever clamorous for more, and they afford no rest. The outward world of pleasure, personal contact, and noisy activities is a sphere of wear and tear which necessitates the counterbalancing effect of solitude. Just as the body requires rest for the recuperation of its forces, so the spirit requires solitude for the renewal of its energies. Solitude is as indispensable to man's spiritual welfare as sleep is to his bodily well-being; and pure thought, or meditation, which is evoked in solitude, is to the spirit what activity is to the body. As the body breaks down when deprived of the needful rest and sleep, so do the spirits of men break down, being deprived of the necessary silence and solitude. Man, as a spiritual being, cannot be maintained in strength, uprightness, and peace except he periodically withdraw himself from the outer world of perishable things and reach inwardly toward the abiding and imperishable realities. The consolations of the creeds are derived from the solitude which those creeds enforce. The regular observance of the ceremonies of formal religion, attended, as they are, with concentrated silence and freedom from worldly distractions, compels men to do unconsciously that which they have not yet learned to do consciously—namely, to concentrate the mind periodically on the inward silence, and meditate, though very briefly, on high and holy things. The man who has not learned to control and purify his mind in seasons of chosen solitude, yet whose awakening aspirations grope for something higher and nobler than he yet possesses, feels the necessity for the aid of ceremonial religion; but he who has taken himself in hand with a view to self-conquest, who withdraws into solitude in order to grapple with his lower nature, and masterfully bend his mind in holy directions, requires no further aid from book or priest or Church. The Church does not exist for the pleasure of the saint but for the elevation of the sinner.

In solitude a man gathers strength to meet the difficulties and temptations of life, knowledge to understand and conquer them, and wisdom to transcend them. As a building is preserved and sustained by virtue of the foundation which is hidden and unobserved, so a man is maintained perpetually in strength and peace by virtue of his lonely hour of intense thought which no eye beholds.

It is in solitude only that a man can be truly revealed to himself, that he can come to understand his real nature, with all its powers and possibilities. The voice of the spirit is not heard in the hubbub of the world and amid the clamors of conflicting desires. There can be no spiritual growth without solitude.

There are those who shrink from too close a scrutiny of themselves, who dread too complete a self-revelation, and who fear that solitude which would leave them alone with their own thoughts and call up before their mental vision the wraith of their desires. And so they go where the din of pleasure is loudest and where the reproving voice of Truth is drowned. But he who loves Truth, who desires and seeks wisdom, will be much alone. He will seek the fullest, clearest revelation of himself, will avoid the haunts of frivolity and noise, and will go where the sweet, tender voice of the spirit of Truth can speak within him and be heard.

Men go after much company, and seek out new excitements, but they are not acquainted with peace; in divers paths of pleasure they search for happiness, but they do not come to rest; through diverse ways of laughter and feverish delirium they wander after gladness and life, but their tears are many and grievous, and they do not escape death.

Drifting upon the ocean of life in search of selfish indulgences men are caught in its storms, and only after many tempests and much privation do they fly to the Rock of Refuge which rests in the deep silence of their own being.

While a man is absorbed in outward activities he is giving out his energies, and is becoming spiritually weaker, and in order to retain his moral vigor he must resort to solitary meditation. So needful is this that he who neglects it loses or does not attain the right knowledge of life; nor does he comprehend and overcome those most deeply-rooted and subtlest of sins which appear like virtues, deceiving the elect, and to which all but the truly wise succumb.

> *True dignity abides with him alone,*
> *Who, in the silent hour of inward thought,*
> *Can still suspect and still revere himself*
> *In lowliness of heart.*

He who lives, without ceasing, in outward excitement lives most in disappointments and griefs. Where the sounds of pleasure are great-est heart-emptiness is the keenest and deepest. He, also, whose whole life, even if not one of lust for pleasure, is centered in outward works, who deals only with the changing panorama of visi-ble things, never falling back, in solitude, upon the inner and invisible world of permanent being, such a man does not attain knowledge and wis-dom, but remains empty; he cannot aid the world, cannot feed its aspirations, for he has no food to offer it, his spiritual store being empty. But he who courts solitude in order to search for the truth of things, who subdues his senses and makes quiet his desires, such a man is daily attaining knowl-edge and wisdom; he becomes filled with the spirit of truth; he can aid the world, for his spiritual store is full, and is kept well replenished.

While a man is absorbed in the contemplation of inward realities he is receiving knowledge and power; he opens himself, like a flower, to the uni-versal light of Truth, and receives and drinks in its life-imparting rays; he also goes to the eternal fountain of knowledge and quenches his thirst in its inspiring waters. Such a man gains, in one hour of concentrated thought, more essential knowl-edge than a whole year's reading could impart. Being is Infinite, and knowledge is illimitable and its source inexhaustible, and he who draws upon the innermost depths of his being drinks from the spring of divine wisdom which can never run dry, and quaffs the waters of immortality.

It is this habitual association with the deep realities of Being, this continual drinking in of the Water of Life at its perennial source, that constitutes *genius*. The resources of genius are inexhaustible because they are drawn from the original and universal source, and for the same reason the works of genius are ever new and fresh. The more a genius gives out the fuller he becomes. With the accomplishment of every work his mind extends and expands, reaches out more vastly, and sees wider and ever wider ranges of power. The genius is inspired. He has bridged the gulf between the finite and the Infinite. He needs no secondary aids, but draws from that universal spring which is the source of every noble work. The difference between a genius and an ordinary man is this— the one lives in inward realities, the other in outward appearances; the one goes after pleasure, the other after wisdom; the one relies on books, the other relies upon his own being. Book-learning is good when its true place is understood, but it is not the source of wisdom. The source of wisdom is in life itself, and is comprehended by effort, practice, and experience. Books give information but they cannot bestow knowledge; they can stimulate but cannot accomplish—you must put forth effort, and achieve for yourself. The man who relies entirely upon books, and does not go to the silent resources within himself, is superficial, and becomes rapidly exhausted. He is uninspired (though he may be extremely clever), for he soon reaches the end of his stock of information, and so becomes void and repetitious. His work lacks the sweet spontaneity of life and the ever-renewed freshness of inspiration. Such a man has cut himself off from the Infinite supply, and deals, not with life itself, but with dead or decaying appearances. Information is limited; knowledge is boundless.

The inspiration of genius and greatness is fostered, evolved, and finally completed in solitude. The most ordinary man who conceives a noble purpose, and, summoning all his energies and will, broods upon and ripens his purpose in solitude will accomplish his object and become a genius. The man who renounces the pleasures of the world, who avoids popularity and fame, and who works in obscurity and thinks in solitude for the accomplishment of a lofty ideal for the human race, becomes a seer and a prophet. He who silently sweetens his heart, who attunes his mind to that which is pure and beautiful and good, who in long hours of lonely contemplation strives to reach to the central and eternal heart of things, brings himself in touch with the inaudible harmonies of being, opens himself for the reception of the cosmic song, and becomes at last a singer and a poet.

And so with all genius: it is the child of solitude—a very simple-hearted child—wide-eyed and listening and beautiful, yet withal to the noise-enamored world an incomprehensible mystery, of which it is only now and then vouchsafed a glimpse from beyond the well-guarded Portals of Silence.

> *In man's self arise*
> *August anticipations, symbols, types*
> *Of a dim splendor ever on before*
> *In that eternal circle life pursues.*

St. Paul, the cruel persecutor and blind bigot, after spending three years alone in the desert, comes forth a loving apostle and an inspired seer. Gautama Siddartha, the man of the world, after six years (in the forest) of lonely struggle with his passions and intense meditation upon the deep mysteries of his nature, becomes Buddha, the enlightened one, the embodiment of calm, serene wisdom, to whom a heart-thirsty world turns to receive the refreshing waters of immortality. Lao-Tze, an ordinary citizen filling a worldly office, in his search for knowledge courts solitude, and discovers Tao, the

Supreme Reason, by virtue of which he becomes a world-teacher. Jesus, the unlettered carpenter, after many years of solitary communion upon the mountains with the Unfailing Love and Wisdom, comes forth a blessed savior of mankind.

Even after they had attained, and had scaled the lofty heights of divine knowledge these Great Souls were much alone, and retired frequently for brief seasons of solitude. The greatest man will fall from his moral height and lose his influence if he neglects that renewal of power which can only be obtained in solitude. These Masters attained their power by consciously harmonising their thoughts and lives with the creative energies within themselves, and by transcending individuality and sinking their petty personal will in the Universal Will they became Masters of Creative Thought, and stand as the loftiest instruments for the outworking of cosmic evolution.

And this is not miraculous, it is a matter of law; it is not mysterious except in so far as law is mysterious. Every man becomes a creative master in so far as he subordinates himself to the universally good and true. Every poet, painter, saint, and sage is the mouthpiece of the Eternal. The perfection of the message varies with the measure of individual selfishness. In so far as self intervenes the distinctness of the work and message becomes blurred.

Perfect selfishness is the acme of genius, the con-summation of power.

Such self-abnegation can only be begun, pur-sued, and completed in solitude. A man cannot gather together and concentrate his spiritual forces while he is engaged in spending those forces in worldly activities, and although after power is attained the balance of forces can be maintained under all circumstances, even in the midst of the antagonistic throng, such power is only secured after many years of frequent and habitual solitude.

Man's true Home is in the Great Silence—this is the source of all that is real and abiding within him; his present nature, however, is dual, and outer activities are necessary. Neither entire soli-tude nor entire action is the true life in the world, but that is the true life which gathers, in solitude, strength and wisdom to rightly perform the activi-ties of life; and as a man returns to his home in the evening, weary with labor, for that sweet rest and refreshment which will prepare him for another day's toil, so must he who would not break down in the labor of life come away from the noise and toil of the world's great workshop and rest for brief periods in his abiding Home in the Silence. He who does this, spending some portion of each day in sacred and purposeful solitude, will become strong and useful and blessed.

Solitude is for the strong, or for those who are ready to become strong. When a man is becoming great he becomes solitary. He goes in solitude to seek, and that which he seeks he finds, for there is a Way to all knowledge, all wisdom, all truth, all power. And the Way is forever open, but it lies through soundless solitudes and the unexplored silences of man's being.

Standing Alone

By all means use to be alone.
Salute thyself; see what thy soul doth wear.
                              –George Herbert

He that has light within his own clear breast
May sit in the centre and enjoy bright day.
                              –Milton

In the life of blessedness self-reliance is of the utmost importance. If there is to be peace there must be strength; if there is to be security there must be stability; if there is to be lasting joy there must be no leaning upon things which at any moment may be snatched away forever.

A man does not begin truly to live until he finds an immovable centre within himself on which to stand, by which to regulate his life, and from which to draw his peace. If he trusts to that which fluctuates he also will fluctuate; if he leans upon that which may be withdrawn he will fall and be bruised; if he looks for satisfaction in perishable accumulations he will starve for happiness in the midst of plenty.

Let a man learn to stand alone, looking to no one for support; expecting no favors, craving no personal advantages; not begging nor complaining, not craving nor regretting, but relying upon the truth within himself, deriving his satisfaction and comfort from the integrity of his own heart.

If a man can find no peace within himself where shall he find it? If he dreads to be alone with himself what steadfastness shall he find in company? If he can find no joy in communion with his own thoughts, how shall he escape misery in his contact with others? The man who has yet found nothing within himself upon which to stand will nowhere find a place of constant rest.

Men everywhere are deluded by thc superstition that their happiness rests with other people and with outward things, and, as a result, they live in continual disappointments, regrets, and lamentations. The man who does not look for happiness to any others or to external things, but finds within himself its inexhaustible source, will be self-contained and serene under all circumstances, and will never become the helpless victim of misery and grief. The man who looks to others for support, who measures his happiness by the conduct of others and not by his own, who depends upon their co-operation for his peace of mind—such a man has no spiritual foothold, his mind is tossed hither and thither with the continual changes going on around him, and he lives in that ceaseless ebb and flow of the spirits which is wretchedness and unrest. He is a spiritual cripple, and has yet to learn how to maintain his mental centre of gravity, and so go without the aid of crutches.

As a child learns to walk in order to go about from place to place of itself strong and unaided, so should a man learn to stand alone, to judge and think and act for himself, and to choose, in the strength of his own mind, the pathway which he shall walk.

Without is change and decay and insecurity, within is all surety and blessedness. The soul is sufficient of itself. Where the need is there is the abundant supply. Your eternal dwelling-place is within; go there and take possession of your mansion; there you are a king, elsewhere you are a vassal. Be contented that others shall manage or mismanage their own little kingdom, and see to it that you reign strongly over your own. Your entire well-being and the well-being of the whole world lies there. You have a conscience, follow it; you have a mind, clarify it; you have judgment, use and improve it; you have a will, employ and strengthen it; you have knowledge, increase it; there is a light within your own soul, watch it, tend it, encourage it, shield it from the winds of passion, and help it to burn with a steadier and ever steadier radiance. Leave the world and come back to yourself. Think as a man, act as a man, live as a man. Be rich in yourself, be complete in yourself. Find the abiding centre within you and obey it. The earth is maintained in its orbit by its obedience to its centre the sun. Obey the centre of light that is within you; let others call it darkness if they will. You are responsible for yourself, are accountable to yourself, therefore rely upon yourself. If you fear yourself who will place confidence in you? If you are untrue to yourself where shall you find the sweet satisfaction of Truth?

The great man stands alone in the simple dignity of independent manhood; he pursues his own path fearlessly, and does not apologise or "beg leave." Criticism and applause are no more to him than the dust upon his coat, of which he shakes himself free. He is not guided by the changing opinions of men but guides himself by the light of his own mind. Other men barter away their manhood for messes of flattery or fashion.

Until you can stand alone, looking for guidance neither to spirits nor mortals, gods nor men, but guiding yourself by the light of the truth within you, you are not unfettered and free, not altogether blessed. But do not mistake pride for self-reliance. To attempt to stand upon the crumbling foundation of pride is to be already fallen. No man depends upon others more than the proud man. He drinks in their approbation and resents their censure. He mistakes flattery for sound judgment, and is most easily hurt or pleased by the opinions of others. His happiness is entirely in the hands of others. But the self-reliant man stands, not upon personal pride, but on an abiding law, principle, ideal, reality, within himself. Upon this he poises himself, refusing to be swept from his strong foothold either by the waves of passion within or the storms of opinion without, but should he at any time lose his balance he quickly regains himself, and is fully restored. His happiness is entirely in his own hands.

Find your centre of balance and succeed in standing alone, and, whatever your work in life may be, you will succeed; you will accomplish what you set your mind upon, for the truly self-reliant man is the invincible man. But though you do not rely upon others, learn of them. Never cease to increase in knowledge, and be ever ready to receive that which is good and useful. You cannot have too much humility; the most self-reliant men are the most humble. "No aristocrat, no prince born to the purple, can begin to compare with the self-respect of the saint. Why is he lowly, but that he knows that he can well afford it, resting on the largeness of God in him." Learn of all men, and especially of the masters of Truth, but do not lose your hold upon the truth that the ultimate guidance is in yourself. A master can say: "Here is the path," but he can neither compel you to walk it nor walk it for you. You must put forth your own efforts, must achieve by your own strength, must make his truth your truth by your own unaided exertions; you must implicitly trust yourself.

This thing is God—to be man with thy might,
To grow great in the strength of thy spirit,
And live out thy life as the light.

You are to be master of yourself, lord over yourself, not fawning and imitating, but doing your work as a living, vital portion of the universe; giving love but not expecting it; giving sympathy but not craving for it; giving aid but not depending upon it. If men should censure your work, heed them not. It sufficeth that your work be true: rest you in this sufficiency. Do not ask: "Will my work please?" but: "Is it real?" If your work be true the criticism of men cannot touch it; if it be false their disapproval will not slay it quicker than it will die of itself. The words and acts of Truth cannot pass away until their work is fully accomplished; the words and acts of error cannot remain, for they have no work to do. Criticism and resentment are alike superfluous.

Free yourself from the self-imposed tyranny of slavish dependence, and stand alone, not as an isolated unit, but as a sympathetic portion of the whole. Find the joy that results from well-earned freedom, the peace that flows from wise self-possession, the blessedness that inheres in native strength.

Honor to him who, self-complete, if lone,
Carves to the grave one pathway all his own,
And heeding naught that men may think or say,
Asks but his soul if doubtful of the way.

Understanding The Simple Laws of Life

Watch narrowly
The demonstration of a truth, its birth,
And you trace back the effluence to its spring
And source within us.

–Browning

More is the treasure of the Law than gems;
Sweeter than comb its sweetness. Its delights,
Delightful past compare.

–The Light of Asia

Walking those byways which I have so far pointed out, resting in their beauty and drinking in their blessedness, the pilgrim along life's broad highway will in due time come to one wherein his last burden will fall from him, where all his weariness will pass away, where he will drink of light-hearted liberty, and rest in perpetual peace. And this most blessed of spiritual byways, the richest source of strength and comfort, I call *The Right Understanding of the Simple Laws of Life.* He who comes to it leaves behind him all lack and longing, all doubt and perplexity, all sorrow and uncertainty. He lives in the fulness of satisfaction, in light and knowledge, in gladness and surety. He who comprehends the utter simplicity of life, who obeys its laws and does not step aside into the dark paths and complex mazes of selfish desire, stands where no harm can reach him, where no enemy can lay him low—and he doubts, desires, and sorrows no more. Doubt ends where reality begins; painful desire ceases where the fulness of joy is perpetual and complete; and when the Unfailing and Eternal Good is realised what room is there for sorrow?

Human life when rightly lived is simple with a beautiful simplicity, but it is not rightly lived while it is bound to a complexity of lusts, desires, and wants—these are not the real life but the burning fever and painful disease which originate in an unenlightened condition of mind. The curtailing of one's desires is the beginning of wisdom; their entire mastery its consummation. This is so because life is bounded by law, and, being inseparable from law, life has no need that is not already supplied. Now lust, or desire, is not need, but a rebellious superfluity, and as such it leads to deprivation and misery. The prodigal son, while in his father's house, not only had all that he required, but was surrounded with a super-abundance. Desire was not necessary, because all things were at hand; but when desire entered his heart he "went into a far country," and "began to be in want," and it was only when he became reduced to the utmost extremity of starvation that he turned with longing toward his father's home. This parable is symbolical of the evolution of the individual and the race. Man has come into such a complexity of cravings that he lives in con-tinual discontent, dissatisfaction, want, and pain; and his only cure lies in a return to the Father's Home—that is, to actual *living* or *being* as distin-guished from *desiring*. But a man does not do this until he is reduced to the last extremity of spir-itual starvation; he has then reaped the experi-ence of pain and sorrow as the result of desire, and looks back with longing toward the true life of peace and plenty; and so he turns round, and begins his toilsome journey back toward his Home, toward that rich life of simple being wherein is emancipation from the thraldom and fever and hunger of desire, and this longing for the true life, for Truth, Reality, should not be confounded with desire: it is *aspiration*. Desire is *the craving for possession; aspiration is the hunger of the heart for peace.* The craving for things leads ever farther and farther from peace, and not only ends in deprivation but is, in itself, a state of perpetual want. Until it comes to an end rest, satisfaction, is an impossibility. The hunger for things can never be satisfied, but the hunger for peace can, and the satisfaction of peace is found, is fully possessed, when all selfish desire is abandoned. Then there is fulness of joy, abounding plenty, and rich and complete blessedness. In this supremely blessed state life is comprehended in its perfect symmetry and simplicity, and the acme of power and usefulness is attained. Then even the hunger for peace ceases, for peace becomes the normal condition, is fully possessed, constant, and never-varying. Men, immersed in desire, ignorantly imagine that the conquest of desire leads to inactivity, loss of power, and lifelessness. Instead, it leads to highly concentrated activity, to the full employment of power, and to a life so rich, so glorious, and so abundantly blessed as to be incomprehensible to those who hunger for pleasures and possessions. Of this life only can it be said:

Here are no sounds of discord—no profane
Or senseless gossip of unworthy things—
Only the songs of chisels and of pens,
Of busy brushes, and ecstatic strains
Of souls surcharged with music most divine.
Here is no idle sorrow, no poor grief
For any day or object left behind—
For time is counted precious, and herein
Is such complete abandonment of Self
That tears turn into rainbows, and enhance
The beauty of the land where all is fair.

When a man is rescued from selfish desire his mind is unencumbered, and he is free to work for humanity. No longer racing after those gratifications which leave him hungry still, all his powers are at his immediate command. Seeking no rewards he can concentrate all his energies upon the faultless completion of his duties, and so accomplish all things and fulfil all righteousness.

The fully enlightened and fully blessed man is not prompted to action by desire but works from *knowledge*. The man of desire needs the promise of a reward to urge him to action. He is as a child working for the possession of a toy. But the man of knowledge, living in the fulness of life and power, can at any moment bring his energies into requisition for the accomplishment of that which is necessary. He is, spiritually, a full-grown man; for him all rewards have ceased; to him all occurrences are good; he lives always in complete satisfaction. Such a man has attained to life, and his delight (and it is a sweet, perpetual, and never-failing delight) is in obedience to the simple demands of exact and never-failing law.

But this life of supreme blessedness is an end, and the pilgrim who is striving towards it, the prodigal returning to it, must travel thither, and employ means to get there. He must pass through the country of his animal desires, disentangling himself from their intricacies, simplifying them, overcoming them; this is the way, and he has no enemies but what spring within himself.

At first the way seems hard because, blinded by desire, he does not perceive the simple structure of life, and its laws are hidden from him; but as he becomes more simple in his mind the direct laws of life become unfolded to his spiritual perception, and at once the point is reached where these laws begin to be understood and obeyed; then the way becomes plain and easy; there is no more uncertainty and darkness, but all is seen in the clear light of knowledge.

It will help to accelerate the progress of the searcher for the true and blessed life if we now turn to a consideration of some of these simple laws which are rigidly mathematical in their operations.

The elementary laws never apologise.

All life is one, though it has a diversity of manifestations; all law is one, but it is applicable and operative in a variety of ways. There is not one law for matter and another for mind, not one for the material and visible and another for the spiritual and invisible; there is the same law throughout. There is not one kind of logic for the world and another for the spirit, but the same logic is applicable to both. Men faithfully, and with unerring worldly wisdom, observe certain laws or rules of action in material things, knowing that to ignore or disobey them would be great folly on their part, ending in disaster for themselves and confusion for society and the state, but they err in supposing and believing that the same rules do not apply in spiritual things, and thereby suffer for their ignorance and disobedience.

It is a law in worldly things that a man shall support himself, that he shall earn his living, and that "He that will not work, neither shall he eat." Men observe this law, recognising its justice and goodness, and so earn the necessary material sustenance. But in spiritual things men, broadly speaking, deny and ignore the operation of this law. They think that, while it is absolutely just that a man should earn his material bread, and that the man who shirks this law should wander in rags and want, it is right that they should beg for their spiritual bread, think it to be just that they should receive all spiritual blessings without either deserving or attempting to earn them. The result is that most men wander in spiritual beggary and want—that is, in suffering and sorrow—deprived of spiritual sustenance, of joy and knowledge and peace.

If you are in need of any worldly thing—food, clothing, furniture, or other necessary—you do not beg of the store-keeper to give it to you; you ask the price of it, pay for it with your money, and then it becomes your own. You recognise the perfect justice in giving an equivalent for what you receive, and would not wish it to be otherwise. The same just law prevails in spiritual things. If you are in need of any spiritual thing—joy, assurance, peace, or what else soever—you can only come into full possession of it by giving an equivalent; you must pay the price for it. As you must give a portion of your material substance for a worldly thing so you must give a portion of your immaterial substance for a spiritual thing. You must yield up some passion or lust or vanity or indulgence before the spiritual possession can be yours. The miser who clings to his money and will not give up any of it because of the pleasure which its possession affords him cannot have any of the material comforts of life. He lives in continual want and discomfort in spite of all his wealth. The man who will not give up his passions, who clings to anger, unkindness, sensuality, pride, vanity, self-indulgence, for the momentary pleasure which their gratification affords him is a spiritual miser; he cannot have any spiritual comforts, and suffers continual spiritual want and uneasiness in spite of the wealth of worldly pleasures which he fondly hugs and refuses to give up.

The man who is wise in worldly things neither begs nor steals, but labors and purchases, and the world honors him for his uprightness. The man who is wise in spiritual things neither begs nor steals, but labours in his own inner world, and purchases his spiritual possessions. Him the whole universe honours for his righteousness.

It is another law in worldly things that a man who engages himself to another in any form of employment shall be content with the wages upon which he agreed. If at the end of his week's work, and on receiving his wages, he were to ask his employer for a larger sum, pleading that, though he could not justly claim it and did not really deserve it, yet he expected it, he would not only not receive the larger sum but would, doubtless, be discharged from his post. Yet in spiritual things men do not think it to be either foolish or selfish to ask for those blessings—spiritual wages—upon which they never agreed, for which they never labored, and which they do not deserve. Every man gets from the law of the universe that upon which he agrees and for which he works—no more, no less; and he is continually entering into agreements with the Supreme Law—the Master of the universe. For every thought and act which he gives he receives its just equivalent; for all work done in the form of deeds he receives the wages due to him. Knowing this, the enlightened man is always content, always satisfied, and in perfect peace, knowing that whatever he receives (be it what men call misfortune or good fortune) he has earned. The Great Law never cheats any man of his just due, but it says to the railer and the complainer: "Friend, didst thou not agree with me for a penny a day?"

Again, if a man would grow rich in worldly goods he must economise, and husband his financial resources until he has accumulated sufficient capital to invest in some branch of industry; then he must judiciously invest his little store of capital, neither holding it too tightly nor letting it go carelessly. He thus increases both in worldly wisdom and worldly riches. The idle spendthrift cannot grow rich; he is wasteful and riotous. He who would grow rich in spiritual things must also economise, and husband his mental resources. He must curb his tongue and his impulses, not wasting his energy in idle gossip, vain argument, or excesses of temper. In this way he will accumulate a little store of wisdom which is his spiritual capital, and this he must send out into the world for the good of others, and the more he uses it the richer will he become. Thus does a man increase in both heavenly wisdom and heavenly riches. The man who follows his blind impulses and desires and does not control and govern his mind is a spiritual spendthrift: he can never become rich in divine things.

It is a physical law that if we would reach the summit of a mountain we must climb thither. The path must be sought and then carefully followed, and the climber must not give up and go back because of the labour involved and the difficulties to be overcome, nor on account of aching limbs, otherwise his object cannot be accomplished. And this law is also spiritual. He who would reach the high altitudes of moral or intellectual grandeur must climb thither by his own efforts. He must seek out the pathway and then assiduously follow it, not giving up and turning back, but surmounting all difficulties, and enduring for a time trials, temptations, and heartaches, and at last he will stand upon the glorious summit of moral perfection, the would of passion, temptation, and sorrow beneath his feet, and the boundless heavens of divinity stretching vast and silent above his head.

If a man would reach a distant city, or any place of destination, he must travel thither. There is no law by which he can be instantly transported there. He can only get there by putting forth the necessary exertion. If he walks he will put forth great exertion, but it will cost him nothing in money; if he drives or takes train, there will be less actual labor, but he must pay in money for which he has laboured. To reach any place requires labour; this cannot be avoided: it is law. Equally so spiritually. He who would reach any spirtiual destination, such as purity, compassion, wisdom, or peace, must travel thither, and must labour to get there. There is no law by which he can suddenly be transported to any of these beautiful spiritual cities. He must find the most direct route and then put forth the necessary labour, and at last he will come to the end of his journey.

These are but a few of the many laws, or manifestations of the One Great Law, which are to be understood, applied, and obeyed before the full manhood and maturity of spiritual life and blessedness can be attained. There is no worldly or physical law which is not operative, with equal exactness, in the spiritual realm—that is, the inner and invisible world of man's being. Just as physical things are the shadows and types of spiritual realities, so worldly wisdom is the reflected image of Divine Wisdom. All those simple operations of human life in worldly things which men never question, but follow and obey implicitly because of their obvious plainness and exactness, obtain in spiritual things with the same unerring accuracy; and when this is understood, and these laws are as implicitly obeyed in spiritual as in worldly matters, then has a man reached the firm standing-ground of exact knowledge; his sorrows are at an end, and he can doubt no more.

Life is uninvolved, uncompromising justice; its operations are simple, invincible logic. Law reigns forever, and the heart of law is love. Favoritism and caprice are the reverse of both law and love. The universe has no favorites; it is supremely just, and gives to every man his rightful earnings. All is good because all is according to law, and because all is according to law, man can find the right way in life, and, having found it, can rejoice and be glad. The Father of Jesus is the Unfailing Good which is embodied in the law of things. "No evil can happen to a good man either in life or death." Jesus recognised the good in his own fate, and exonerated all his persecutors from blame. "No man," he declared, "taketh my life from me, but I lay it down of myself." That is, he himself had brought about his own end.

He who has, by simplifying his life and purifying his mind, arrived at an understanding of the beautiful simplicity of being, perceives the unvarying operation of law in all things, and knows the result of all his thoughts and deeds upon himself and the world—knows what effects are bound up with the mental causes which he sets in motion. He then thinks and does only those thoughts and deeds that are blessed in their inception, blessed in their growth, and blessed in their completion. Humbly accepting the lawful results of all the deeds done when in a state of ignorance, he neither complains nor fears nor questions, but is at rest in obedience, is perfectly blessed in his knowledge of the Good Law.

> The tissue of our life to be
>   We weave with colors all our own,
> And in the field of Destiny
>   We reap as we have sown.
>
> And if we reap as we have sown,
>   And take the dole we deal,
> The law of pain is love alone,
>   The wounding is to heal.

Happy Endings

Such is the Law which moves to righteousness,
  Which none at last can turn aside or stay;
The heart of it is Love, the end of it
  Is peace and consummation sweet. Obey.
                              –The Light of Asia

So, haply, when thy task shall end,
  The wrong shall lose itself in right,
And all thy week-day Sabbaths blend
  With the long Sabbath of the Light!
                              –Whittier

Life has many happy endings, because it has much that is noble and pure and beautiful. Although there is much sin and ignorance in the world, many tears, and much pain and sorrow, there is also much purity and knowledge, many smiles, and much healing and gladness. No pure thought, no unselfish deed can fall short of its felic-

itous result, and every such result is a happy consummation.

A pleasant home is a happy ending; a successful life is a happy ending; a task well and faithfully done is a happy ending; to be surrounded by
kind friends is a happy ending. A quarrel put away,
grudges wiped out, unkind words confessed and
forgiven, friend restored to friend—all these are
happy endings. To find that which one has long
and tediously sought; to be restored from tears to
gladness; to awaken in the bright sunlight out of
the painful nightmare of sin; to strike, after much
searching, the Heavenly Way in life—these are,
indeed, blessed consummations.

He who looks for, finds, and enters the byways
which I have indicated will come to this one without seeking it, for his whole life will be filled with
happy endings. He who begins right and continues
right does not need to desire and search for felici-
tous results; they are already at hand; they follow
as consequences: they are the certainties, the realities of life.

There are happy endings which belong solely to
the material world; these are transient, and they
pass away. There are happy endings which belong
to the spiritual world; these are eternal, and they
do not pass away. Sweet are companionships, pleasures, and material comforts, but they change and

fade away. Sweeter still are Purity, Wisdom, and the knowledge of Truth, and these never change nor fade away. Wherever a man goes in this world he can take his worldly possessions with him; but soon he must part company with them, and if he stands upon these alone, deriving all his happiness from them, he will come to a spiritual ending of great emptiness and want. But he who has attained to the possession of spiritual things can never be deprived of his source of happiness: he will never have to part company with it, and wherever he goes in the whole universe he will carry his possessions with him. His spiritual end will be the fulness of joy.

Happy in the Eternal Happiness is he who has come to that Life from which the thought of self is abolished. Already, even now and in this life, he has entered the Kingdom of Heaven, Nirvana, Paradise, the New Jerusalem, the Olympus of Jupiter, the Valhalla of the Gods. He knows the Final Unity of Life, the Great Reality of which these fleeting and changing names are but feeble utterances. He is at rest on the bosom of the Infinite.

Sweet is the rest and deep the bliss of him who has freed his heart from its lusts and hatreds and dark desires; and he who, without any shadow of bitterness or selfishness resting upon him, and looking out upon the world with boundless compassion and love, can breathe, in his inmost heart, the blessing:

Peace unto all living things, making no exceptions or distinctions—such a man has reached that happy ending which can never be taken away, for this is the perfection of life, the fulness of peace, the consummation of Perfect Blessedness.

James Allen:
A Memoir

By Lily L. Allen

from *The Epoch* (February–March 1912)

Unto pure devotion
Devote thyself: with perfect meditation
Comes perfect act, and the right-hearted rise—
More certainly because they seek no gain—
Forth from the bands of body, step by step.
To highest seats of bliss.

James Allen was born in Leicester, England, on November 28th, 1864. His father, at one time a very prosperous manufacturer, was especially fond of "Jim," and before great financial failures overtook him, he would often look at the delicate, refined boy, poring over his books, and would say, "My boy, I'll make a scholar of you."

The Father was a high type of man intellectually, and a great reader, so could appreciate the evident thirst for education and knowledge which he observed in his quiet studious boy.

As a young child he was very delicate and nervous, often suffering untold agony during his school days through the misunderstanding harshness of some of his school teachers, and others with whom he was forced to associate, though he retained always the tenderest memories of others—one or two of his teachers in particular, who no doubt are still living.

He loved to get alone with his books, and many a time he has drawn a vivid picture for me, of the hours he spent with his precious books in his favourite corner by the home fire; his father, whom he dearly loved, in his arm chair opposite also deeply engrossed in his favourite authors. On such evenings he would question his father on some of the profound thoughts that surged through his soul—thoughts he could scarcely form into words—and the father, unable to answer, would gaze at him long over his spectacles, and at last say: "My boy, my boy, you have lived before"—and when the boy eagerly but reverently would suggest an answer to his own question, the father would grow silent and thoughtful, as though he *sensed* the future man and his mission, as he looked at the boy and listened to his words—and many a time he was heard to remark, "Such knowledge comes not in one short life."

There were times when the boy startled those about him into a deep concern for his health, and they would beg him not to *think so much*, and in after years he often smiled when he recalled how his father would say—"Jim, we will have you in the Churchyard soon, if you think so much."

Not that he was by any means unlike other boys where games were concerned. He could play leap-frog and marbles with the best of them, and those who knew him as a man—those who were privileged to meet him at "Bryngoleu"—will remember how he could enter into a game with all his heart. Badminton he delighted in during the summer evenings, or whenever he felt he could.

About three years after our marriage, when our little Nora was about eighteen months old, and he about thirty-three, I realized a great change coming over him, and knew that he was renouncing everything that most men hold dear that he might find Truth, and lead the weary sin-stricken world to Peace. He at that time commenced the practice of rising early in the morning, at times long before daylight, that he might go out on the hills—like One of old—to commune with God, and meditate on Divine things. I do not claim to have understood him fully in those days. The light in which he lived and moved was far too white for my earth-bound eyes to see, and a *sense of it only* was beginning to dawn upon me. But I knew I dare not stay him or hold him back, though at times my woman's heart cried out to do so, waiting him all my own, and not then understanding his divine mission.

Then came his first book, "From Poverty to Power." This book is considered by many his best book. It has passed into many editions, and tens of thousands have been sold all over the world, both authorized and pirated editions, for perhaps no author's works have been more pirated than those of James Allen.

As a private secretary he worked from 9 a.m. to 6 p.m., and used every moment out of office writing his books. Soon after the publication of "From Poverty to Power" came "All These Things Added," and then "As a Man Thinketh," a book perhaps better known and more widely read than any other from his pen.

About this time, too, the "Light of Reason" was founded and he gave up all his time to the work of editing the Magazine, at the same time carrying on a voluminous correspondence with searchers after Truth all over the world. And ever as the years went by he kept straight on, and never once looked back or swerved from the path of holiness. Oh, it was a blessed thing indeed to be the chosen one to walk by the side of his earthly body, and to watch the glory dawning upon him!

He took a keen interest in many scientific subjects, and always eagerly read the latest discovery in astronomy, and he delighted in geology and botany. Among his favourite books I find Shakespeare, Milton, Emerson, Browning, The Bhagavad-Gita, the Tao-Tea-King of Lao-Tze, the Light of Asia, the Gospel of Buddha, Walt Whitman, Dr. Bucke's Cosmic Consciousness, and the Holy Bible.

He might have written on a wide range of subjects had he chosen to do so, and was often asked for articles on many questions outside his particular work, but he refused to comply, consecrating his whole thought and effort to preach the Gospel of Peace.

When physical suffering overtook him he never once complained, but grandly and patiently bore his pain, hiding it from those around him, and only we who knew and loved him so well, and his kind, tender Doctor, knew how greatly he suffered. And yet he stayed not; still he rose before the dawn to meditate, and commune with God; still he sat at his desk and wrote those words of Light and Life which will ring down through the ages, calling men and women from their sins and sorrows to peace and rest.

Always strong in his complete manhood, though small of stature physically, and as gentle as he was strong, no one ever heard an angry word from those kind lips. Those who served him adored him; those who had business dealings with him trusted and honoured him. Ah! how much my heart prompts me to write of his self-sacrificing life, his tender words, his gentle deeds, his knowledge and his wisdom. But why? Surely there is no need, for do not his books speak in words written by his own hand, and will they not speak to generations yet to come?

About Christmas time I saw the change coming, and understood it not—blind! blind! blind! I could not think it possible that *he* should be taken and *I* left.

But we three—as if we knew—clung closer to each other, and loved one another with a greater love—if that were possible—than ever before. Look at his portrait given with the January "Epoch," and reproduced again in this, and you will see that even then our Beloved, our Teacher and Guide, was letting go his hold on the physical. He was leaving us then, and we didn't know it. Often I had urged him to stop work awhile and rest, but he always gave me the same answer, "My darling, when I stop I must go, don't try to stay my hand."

And so he worked on, until that day, Friday, January 12, 1912, when, about one o'clock he sat down in his chair, and looking at me with a great compassion and yearning in those blessed eyes, he cried out, as he stretched out his arms to me, *"Oh, I have finished, I have finished, I can go no further, I have done."*

Need I say that everything that human aid and human skill could do was done to keep him still with us. Of those last few days I dare scarcely write. How could my pen describe them? And when we knew the end was near, with his dear hands upon my head in blessing, he gave his work and his beloved people into my hands, charging me to bless and help them, until I received the call to give up my stewardship!

"I will help you," he said, "and if I can I shall come to you and be with you often."

Words, blessed words of love and comfort, *for my heart alone* often came from his lips, and a sweet smile ever came over the pale calm face when our little Nora came to kiss him and speak loving words to him, while always the gentle voice breathed the tender words to her—*"My little darling!"*

So calmly, peacefully, quietly, he passed from us at the dawn on Wednesday, January 24, 1912. "Passed from us," did I say? Nay, only the outer garment has passed from our mortal vision. He lives! and when the great grief that tears our hearts at the separation is calmed and stilled, I think that we shall know that he is still with us. We shall again rejoice in his companionship and presence.

When his voice was growing faint and low, I heard him whispering, and leaning down to catch the words I heard—"At last, at last—at home— my wanderings are over"—and then, I heard no more, for my heart was breaking within me, and I felt, for *him* indeed it was "*Home at last!*" but for me—And then, as though he knew my thoughts, he turned and again holding out his hands to me, he said: "I have only one thing more to say to you, my beloved, and that is I love you, and I will be waiting for you; good-bye."

I write this memoir for those who love him, for those who will read it with tender loving hearts, and tearful eyes; for those who will not look critically at the way in which I have tried to tell out of my lonely heart this short story of his life and passing away—for *his* pupils, and, therefore, my friends.

We clothed the mortal remains in *pure white linen*, symbol of his fair, pure life, and so, clasping the photo of the one he loved best upon his bosom—they committed all that remained to the funeral pyre.

About the Author

James Allen was one of the pioneering figures of the self-help movement and modern inspirational thought. A philosophical writer and poet, he is best known for his book *As a Man Thinketh*. Writing about complex subjects such as faith, destiny, love, patience, and religion, he had the unique ability to explain them in a way that is simple and easy to comprehend. He often wrote about cause and effect, as well as overcoming sadness, sorrow and grief.

Allen was born in 1864 in Leicester, England into a working-class family. His father travelled alone to America to find work, but was murdered within days of arriving. With the family now facing economic disaster, Allen, at age 15, was forced to leave school and find work to support them.

During stints as a private secretary and stationer, he found that he could showcase his spiritual and social interests in journalism by writing for the magazine *The Herald of the Golden Age.*

In 1901, when he was 37, Allen published his first book, *From Poverty to Power.* In 1902 he began to publish his own spiritual magazine, *The Light of Reason* (which would be retitled *The Epoch* after his death). Each issue contained announcements, an editorial written by Allen on a different subject each month, and many articles, poems, and quotes written by popular authors of the day and even local, unheard of authors.

His third and most famous book *As a Man Thinketh* was published in 1903. The book's minor popularity enabled him to quit his secretarial work and pursue his writing and editing career full time. He wrote 19 books in all, publishing at least one per year while continuing to publish his magazine, until his death. Allen wrote when he had a message—one that he had lived out in his own life and knew that it was good.

In 1905, Allen organized his magazine subscribers into groups (called "The Brotherhood") that would meet regularly and reported on their meetings each month in the magazine. Allen and his wife, Lily Louisa Oram, whom he had married in 1895, would often travel to these group meetings to give speeches and read articles. Some of Allen's favorite writings, and those he quoted often, include the works of Shakespeare, Milton, Emerson, the Bible, Buddha, Whitman, Trine, and Lao-Tze.

Allen died in 1912 at the age of 47. Following his death, Lily, with the help of their daughter, Nora took over the editing of *The Light of Reason*, now under the name *The Epoch*. Lily continued to publish the magazine until her failing eyesight prevented her from doing so. Lily's life was devoted to spreading the works of her husband until her death at age 84.

Printed in the USA
CPSIA information can be obtained
at www.ICGtesting.com
JSHW012030140824
68134JS00033B/2973